TWELVE MAKERS OF MODERN
PROTESTANT THOUGHT

Twelve Makers of Moder

NEW YORK

Protestant Thought

EDITED WITH INTRODUCTION

BY *George L. Hunt*

ASSOCIATION PRESS

The following articles in this book are abridged from *Crossroads,* a study and program magazine for adults, published by the Board of Christian Education of the Presbyterian Church in the U.S.A., copyright by W. L. Jenkins, and used by permission of the authors and the publisher:

    Albert Schweitzer (copyright 1955)
    Walter Rauschenbusch (copyright 1957)
    Sören Kierkegaard (copyright 1956)
    Karl Barth (copyright 1956)
    Reinhold Niebuhr (copyright 1956)
    Paul Tillich (copyright 1957)

The other articles have been written expressly for this book.

Standard Book Number: 8096-1824-9

Library of Congress Catalog Card Number: 70-152897

To my son Larry
with the hope that some of these "makers"
will help shape his life and thought as
they have shaped mine.

Contents

Introduction

From the Sixties into the Seventies

BY GEORGE L. HUNT

In 1958 Association Press published a book which I edited, entitled *Ten Makers of Modern Protestant Thought*. Twelve years later I have revised that book, eliminating two of the chapters (those on Emil Brunner and William Temple) and adding four new ones: the ones on Dietrich Bonhoeffer, Jurgen Molt-mann, Martin Heidegger, and Alfred North White-head.

The condition of Protestant theology in 1970 as compared with 1958 is uncertain if not chaotic. In the Fifties there were theological giants in the land, including some of the eight men carried over into this book. Today we see no men on the scene whom we can confidently describe as the heirs of Barth, Niebuhr, and Tillich.

Why is this so? Kenneth Keniston, in a book review, asks the same question in another discipline, and replies: "It is unlikely today that history will again allow us men like Marx and Freud. Events now move too fast for an individual genius to found

GEORGE L. HUNT is Senior Minister, Fanwood Presbyterian Church, Fanwood, New Jersey.

a movement based upon the slow unfolding of his own ideas. The speedup of modern history makes most men's ideas obsolete during their lifetimes, while the instant consumption of both men and ideas by the media effectively prevents that lengthy period of gestation that characterized the great intellectual innovators and movements of the past. At best, what we can hope for today is the development of a new mood of social analysis and criticism that will be the work of many, not one genius." [1]

Could the same be said of Protestant theology today? Who knows? It is perhaps significant that of the four additions to this book only Moltmann is still likely to produce new developments in his thought. Three of our four new "makers" are from the past, although of course there are and will be theologians building upon the work of these men.

The decade of the 1960's has not been marked by fresh and original theological insights because it has (and appropriately so) been an activist decade. The names that come to mind are shakers and doers, not original thinkers: Bishop John Robinson, Harvey Cox, Martin Luther King, Jr., Pope John XXIII, Eugene Carson Blake, and so on.

In my opinion, the past ten years is bounded on the one end by the discovery of Bonhoeffer and on the other end by the possibilities of process theology (i.e., Whitehead). In between we have lived through (and are still in) three crises which have given the tone and posed the problem for this decade.

[1] Kenneth Keniston, *The New York Times Book Review,* September 6, 1970, p. 20.

Three Crises

The three crises are: a loss of meaning and purpose for the church, a crisis in belief, and a crisis in authority. This is the analysis made of the 1960's by Professor Jeffrey K. Hadden in his recent book. Professor Hadden teaches sociology at Tulane University, New Orleans; and in 1965 he conducted an extensive study of the views of 10,000 clergymen on a variety of topics. He also utilized the Glock-Stark study of the views of laymen. After comparing the results of these and other research in the sociology of religion, Professor Hadden concluded that "the Christian churches today are in the midst of a struggle which has every evidence of being the most serious ferment in Christendom since the Protestant Reformation" [2] and that the crisis upon us "may seriously disrupt or alter the very nature of the church." [3] There is a widening gap between the clergy and laymen of the church on matters of purpose and meaning, doctrine, and authority.

Let us look at these three dimensions of crisis in order to put the men included in this book in perspective.

The conflict over *the purpose and meaning* of the church has centered in the church's involvement in social action, most particularly the civil rights struggle. Social action is "where it's at" for the church as it enters the 1970's. The crisis arises over both means and ends and the intensity of the conflict. There are those who think the church has no business getting involved, as the church corporate, in any social

[2] Jeffrey K. Hadden, *The Gathering Storm in the Church* (Doubleday Anchor Book, 1970), p. 3.
[3] *Ibid.,* p. 5.

problem; others would feel that the church should
be involved, but would disagree on how. The militancy of church participation, or, to turn the phrase
around, clergy and church participation in militancy
and violence to effect social change, while not as
widespread as all the publicity would lead us to
think, has created serious disagreement and con-
fusion about the purpose and meaning of the church.
The church is polarized on this issue, and active lay
groups are forming in major Protestant denomina-
tions to change the direction of their social education
and action.

Dietrich Bonhoeffer is the seminal thinker who,
more than any other single Protestant theologian, has
influenced the social action orientation of the church
in this period. It is well-known that his followers
have built upon meager resources: the reflections of
a man in prison (*Letters and Papers from Prison,*
also called *Prisoner for God*) and the beginning of
a book on ethics, never completed.[4] The enigmatic
nature of his statements, and his martyrdom, have
contributed greatly to his appeal.

The word for this new involvement is "secularity."
There was a time when secular was a profane word
in religious circles: it meant life organized apart from
God. But now it is the "in" word; for example,
books with such titles as *The Secular City* (Harvey
Cox) or *The Secular Meaning of the Gospel* (Paul
Van Buren) were popular in the Sixties. What does
the word mean today? "By secular," writes Langden
Gilkey,[5] "I mean here a theology fundamentally

---

[4] It is, however, published. See Dietrich Bonhoeffer, *Ethics*
(SCM Press, 1955). It was written between 1940 and 1943
and first published in Germany in 1949.
[5] Langden Gilkey, "Theology in the Seventies," *Theology
Today,* October 1970, p. 294.

oriented to the secular world in which we exist, a world which for good or ill largely forms us in life and thought, in our sense of reality, of truth, and of value." "A secular theology," he goes on, "I contrast to any theology that moves us away from that world to another sacred realm, place, or authority. If we are anywhere to hear a voice that is not our own—and I believe we must—we hear it *in* that world among its possibilities and upheavals, and enact it in the politics and the crises of that world. This theme has been the dominating, determining force in the theology of the past half decade. I see, and wish to see, no sign of its early weakening."

If theology has been—and may continue to be—increasingly secular, it is easy to see why the average Christian in the pews is confused. Having been taught to believe in a transcendent God, omnipotent, and all the rest, and now to be told that God is "in the world"—which then becomes the theological justification for activism—it is understandable why there should be this crisis in meaning and purpose. The old serenities and securities of both religion and culture have been shaken. The shaking of the foundation can lead to renewal and re-creation, but it is tough living through the earthquake!

The *crisis in belief* relates, obviously, to the crisis in meaning and purpose. If you do not have a sense of purpose it is because your fundamental beliefs have eroded or been attacked.

What is this crisis of belief? Professor Hadden enumerates the statistics from various surveys as well as the response to such books as Bishop Robinson's *Honest to God*. Published in May 1963, it is considered by some historians of contemporary religious thought to mark the end of the old era and the beginning of the new.[6] Concerning the response to *Honest to God* among laymen, Hadden says, "To some laymen the appearance of *Honest to God* was a refreshing revelation. But to others it was a shocking confirmation of what they had long suspected—that theologians had abandoned the most fundamental doctrines which have been held to be the very basis of the Christian heritage." [7] He then goes on to quote some statistics:

"Among the Protestant laity in the Glock and Stark study, 29 per cent had at least some doubts about the existence of God, 43 per cent were not completely convinced that Jesus was born of a virgin, and 35 per cent had some doubt as to the possibility of a life beyond death. Among Congregationalists, the most liberal denomination in the study, the proportion who expressed doubt regarding fundamental orthodox beliefs ran much higher. Fifty-nine per cent had some doubts about the existence of God, 79 per cent expressed some doubt about the virgin conception of Jesus, and 64 per cent were not altogether certain that there is a life after death.

"Clergy have the same difficulty accepting orthodox Christian doctrine. Twenty-six per cent of the clergy are not completely convinced that the birth of Jesus was a biological miracle, and 18 per cent cannot affirm the doctrine of divine judgment after death where some will be rewarded and others punished. Perhaps even more important is the fact that 62 per cent of the clergy indicate that they would expect a *thinking* Christian to have doubts about the exis-

---

[6] See Brevard S. Childs, *Biblical Theology in Crisis* (Westminster Press, 1970), p. 85.

[7] Hadden, *op. cit.,* p. 20.

tence of God; with doubt comes rejection of certain specific doctrines." [8]

Along with this doubt, says Hadden, has come a decline in church attendance which reflects the three-fold crisis. In 1955, according to a Gallup Poll, 49 per cent of the respondents attended church in an average week. In 1966 it was 44 per cent. We can be reasonably certain it is even less today. Another statistic is also interesting. In response to the question, "At the present time, do you think religion as a whole is increasing its influence on American life, or losing its influence?", the Gallup Poll found in 1957 69 per cent said it was increasing and only 14 per cent said it was losing its influence; in 1967 the figures were dramatically reversed: 23 per cent increasing, 57 per cent losing. Of course, what you mean by "influence," in this type of poll, is a subjective matter. Yet the opinion itself is significant.

What are the options for resolving this crisis in belief? One would be a return to orthodoxy, perhaps a chastened, more sophisticated orthodoxy, but nevertheless a reaffirmation of the historic biblical faith. We need only recall that the "secularity" and social gospel of the period from 1910 to 1930 was followed by the neo-orthodoxy of the 1940's and '50's. Reinhold Niebuhr's social action vigorously informed by a biblical faith met the needs of these decades. Who is to say that it cannot happen again?

A sign in this direction may be the new book by Brevard S. Childs, of the Yale Divinity School. After reviewing the Biblical Theology Movement of the past twenty-five years and describing its demise, he asserts, "The threat of a new American theological liberalism that finds its warrant for social action in a vague reference to 'making human the structures

[8] *Ibid.,* pp. 23–4.

of society' has already made strong inroads into the life of the church. Biblical Theology would seem to have a decisive role to play in meeting this challenge at this time." [9] Childs then makes his case for a new biblical theology which will be built around "the canon of the Christian Church as the most appropriate context from which to do Biblical Theology." [10] "By taking seriously the canon," he writes later on, "one confesses along with the church to the unique function that these writings have had in its life and faith as Sacred Scripture. Then each new generation of interpreters seeks to be faithful in searching these Scriptures for renewed illumination while exploiting to the fullest the best tools available for opening the texts. Ultimately, to stand within the tradition of the church is a stance not made in the spirit of dogmatic restriction of the revelation of God, but in joyful wonder and even surprise as the Scripture becomes the bread of life for another generation." [11]

A second option that might meet the crisis in belief would grow out of the religiosity of the present college generation. (See *The Making of a Counter-Culture* by Theodore Roszak.) The emphasis on emotion, feeling; the search for meaning in drugs and esoteric religions; the intense concern about war, pollution, etc.; the development of a distinctive life-style—who knows where these may lead in shaping the faith of the next decades? Perhaps all we can say at this point is that we must be aware of the religious undertones present in the searching of youth today, listen for them, respond to them, and possibly redirect them if we should and where we can.[12]

[9] Childs, *op. cit.,* p. 94.

[10] *Ibid.,* p. 99.

[11] *Ibid.,* p. 107.

[12] *Time* magazine for November 2, 1970 comments: "The groping of the young toward a natural piety and spiritual

A third option is process theology. We represent this direction of thought here with the essay on A. N. Whitehead. It is not that I, the editor, think process theology will be the wave of the future. It is only that Whitehead's philosophy seems to be the dominant influence on the scholars who are doing the most creative work of theological reconstruction at this time: John Cobb, Schubert Ogden, Norman Pittenger, and Daniel Day Williams. These are the men who "have seen in the new metaphysics [of process philosophy] a possibility for rethinking the theological doctrine of God in relation to a contemporary view of nature and the new historical consciousness." [13]

Process thought or philosophy is difficult to summarize. Professor Cobb's essay should be read and reflected on very carefully. Perhaps the greatest challenge of Whitehead's philosophy to Christian theology lies in the way it leads us to rethink the activity of God. It is obvious that our ideas and activities as men are always in process, always developing; but we have not been accustomed to say the same thing about God. Yet if, as process philosophy claims, "reality is not made up of unchanging substances, which have 'accidental' relationships, but of processes, or events, or 'occasions of experience' that have relatively enduring abstract structures or forms"; [14] and if God is reality, "the supreme exemplification rather than the contradiction of meta-

---

brotherhood in a time admittedly cut off from religion and nature may possibly be the single most significant struggle in recent U. S. history" (p. 13).

[13] Daniel Day Williams, *The Spirit and the Forms of Love* (Harper and Row, 1968), p. 105.

[14] "Process Philosophy" in Van A. Harvey, *A Handbook of Theological Terms* (Macmillan, 1964), p. 191.

physical principles required to explain the world"; [15]
then "God is affected by that which occurs in the
created order, for what happens enters into his life
and influences his 'decisions' by providing new possibilities for his future activity." [16]

Norman Pittenger charts a course for process
theology when he writes: "What is needed today, I
believe, is the radical attempt to work out a theological pattern for Christian faith which is in the main
influenced by process-philosophy, while at the same
time use is made of what we have been learning
from the existentialist's insistence on engagement and
decision, the understanding of history as involving
genuine participation and social context, and the
psychologist's awareness of the depths of human
emotional, conational, and rational experience. It is
to be hoped that those who engage in the task will
remember that this attempt would necessarily be an
essay in reconception, making no pretense to being
conclusive or exhaustive. But a considerable number
of such experiments would be of great value in
furthering the perennial task of thinking-through
once again what it means to 'confess that Jesus
Christ is Lord, to the glory of God the Father.'" [17]

This task of reconstruction is now going on. The
student interested in joining the search party on its
journey of exploration may read some of the books
mentioned in the notes to these paragraphs as well
as those listed at the end of the Whitehead essay.

The third crisis is the *crisis of authority.* "In the
past," writes Professor Hadden, "laity have not ob-

---

[15] Norman Pittenger, *Process Thought and Christian Faith*
(Macmillan, 1968), p. 29.
[16] *Ibid.,* p. 29.
[17] *Ibid.,* p. 94.

jected seriously to the authority structure of their churches. To the extent that they have even been aware of the fact that the clergy were calling most of the shots, they have not been particularly disturbed. But when the rank and file of a voluntary association object to the direction in which the leadership is moving the organization, they begin to exercise their own authority. In Protestantism today, laity, who have entrusted authority to professional leaders, have come to have grave doubts about how the authority has been used, and are beginning to assert their own influence." [18]

Hadden's research centers in the church's response to the civil rights crisis of the 1960's. But the response to this problem may well be the harbinger for things to come. On the part of the young and the disenchanted, this crisis has taken the form of strong anti-institutionalism. On the part of many adults, it has resulted in either determined efforts to change the direction in which the church is going or drastic cuts in church giving, especially to national agencies.

Where *is* Protestantism going in its attitude toward the authority of the church and in the future effectiveness of the church? More particularly, we may wonder, for the purposes of this book, what ecclesiology, what doctrine of the church, is likely to emerge in the future?

Langden Gilkey's cautious prognostications about the ecumenical theology of the 1970's has some relevance at this point, for the broadening of theology out of denominational slots into ecumenical perspectives will have some long-range implications for a doctrine of the church. He writes: "Protestant theology will, and must, be vividly and vitally strengthened by its new relations to Roman Catholic thought.

[18] Hadden, *op. cit.,* pp. 33–4.

One can now, and surely in the future, find and only speak of *Christian* theology, not of Protestant or Roman Catholic theology. These latter labels will, I hazard, become as anachronistic as labels as are Presbyterian or Congregational theology today; and Karl Rahner and Bernard Lonergan will be read as naturally and as widely as are now Barth and Tillich. The relations of Christian theology to other religions will surely be a major concern for us all. Our world, our horizons, and hence our cultures now interpenetrate; each of us, therefore, is seeking to deal with the *same* world of modernity. In so far as each offers itself as providing a religious interpretation of the same cultural world, our dialogue, if not our competition, is bound to increase. An ecumenical movement of religions is on its way. Probably the hardest ecumenical challenge will be between white and black theology, now moving unhappily into different spiritual orbits. Ecumenical growth and healing here will follow political and not theological changes. For it has been our moral and political failures, not theological dogmas, that have caused the present schism." [19]

It is also likely that the proposed Church of Christ Uniting, about which some decision should have been made by 1979, will have some influence on the problem of authority. The structure for the united church outlined in its Plan of Union [20] allows for episcopal, presbyteral, and lay authority in a synthesis unlike anything now in existence. Bishops will

[19] Gilkey, *loc. cit.*, pp. 293–4.
[20] See *A Plan of Union for the Church of Christ Uniting* (Princeton, Consultation on Church Union, 1970). The relation of bishops to councils is described on pp. 51–2; on council representation, see p. 61; on the place of minorities in leadership, see the basic structural principle on p. 11 and an illustration of a united church at work on pp. 58–9.

have their authority circumscribed by councils; on
the councils laity will outnumber ordained bishops
and presbyters two to one. Great stress is placed on
the ministry of all believers; precise provision is made
for minority groups in the leadership of the church.
Power and authority have a new geographical locus:
away from the congregation to the parish (a combination of congregations), away from the national
level to the region and district. The implications of
these structural matters for the future of theological
thought may be negligible; on the other hand, since
nineteenth-century denominationalism had a great
effect on nineteenth-century theology, who is to say
that twentieth-century attempts at church union will
not eventually be equally influential? At any rate,
the Church of Christ Uniting may be one of the significant arenas where the crisis in church authority
will have to be dealt with in the years ahead.

As the church faces its future it will have to be
with an exodus mentality. It must follow God into a
wilderness, not knowing what the Promised Land is
like, and often longing probably for the fleshpots of
Egypt (i.e., its false prosperity of the Fifties). The
theologian who best speaks to this prospect is Jürgen
Moltmann, as the essay in this book by Daniel Migliore makes clear. Our authority is still God, however we speak of him and however we respond to
where he leads us.

Where Do They All Fit In?

I have chosen the categories of purpose, belief,
and authority to describe the theological situation of
the Sixties and to provide a look into the problems
of the Seventies. Other writers would use other categories. These describe the way I see it, as a pastor
who has lived with, taught, preached to, and learned

from a suburban middle-class congregation in northern New Jersey. These crises are very much upon us; and this book is meant to be a kind of guide through the past with some hesitant steps made into the future. In our zeal to embrace Bonhoeffer we must not forget Barth.

In the introduction to *Ten Makers of Modern Protestant Thought* I categorized the movements of those days under the headings of Bible study, social concern, theology, and the nature and mission of the church, and put the ten "makers" into these slots. Comparing these four categories to my present three, it is instructive to note the shift in emphasis and interest. "Social concern" is covered in this book under "meaning and purpose," and so Rauschenbusch and Niebuhr join Bonhoeffer here. "Theology" is related to "belief," with Barth, Kierkegaard, Tillich, and Buber occupying the same terrain as Heidegger and Whitehead. "Nature and mission of the church" was represented in the earlier book by Temple; in this book its spokesman, under the rubric of "authority," is Moltmann. (The tenuous relationship of either Temple or Moltmann to the categories assigned them speaks volumes and says that in these categories we have more theological problems than theological answers.)

"Bible study" is not one of my headings in 1970, yet it was the first one in 1958. Schweitzer and Bultmann are the "makers" that fit in here. Why is there no new name to add out of the Sixties and as a precursor for the Seventies? One reason is that Bultmann stands for both periods. He is by no means passé. The other is, frankly, that the development in Bible study of the Sixties, known as "the new hermeneutics," has in my opinion not yet achieved a clarity (at least in English translation) or sense of direction which would make an essay on one of its chief exponents, Ernst Fuchs or Wolfhart Pannenberg, useful to the laymen for whom this book is intended.

After the tumult of the past decade one might face the future in a state of exhaustion and anxiety. The crises have taken their toll on those of us who have lived through them, and the end is not yet. But there is still a great deal of life left in the church and among those who are trying to shape the thought (the theology) of the future. It's a great time to be alive!

FOR FURTHER READING

John Dillenberger and Claude Welch, *Protestant Christianity* (New York: Charles Scribner's Sons, 1954). In paperback, Scribner Library.

Robert McAfee Brown, *The Spirit of Protestantism* (Oxford University Press, 1961).

Martin E. Marty, "American Protestant Theology Today" in Dean Peerman, *Front Line Theology* (London: SCM Press) 1967.

Langden Gilkey, *Naming the Whirlwind* (Indianapolis: Bobbs-Merrill, 1969). The most thorough survey of Protestant thought in the Sixties.

See also the works cited in the footnotes.

I

Albert Schweitzer

BY HENRY A. RODGERS

Enthusiastic admirers have called Albert Schweitzer the "greatest man in the world." Whether or not he deserves this superlative title, there is no doubt about the impact made by the force of his personality upon the world of our day.

Born in 1875, he grew up in the little town of Günsbach in the then German, now French province of Alsace. His father was pastor of the Evangelical congregation. At the age of thirty Albert Schweitzer resolved to give his life to some task of service to humanity as an expression of his stewardship to Christ. After considering various projects, he found his call in an advertisement of the Paris Missionary Society for a medical doctor to serve in French Equatorial Africa. He had already earned doctorates in philosophy, theology, and music. To these he now added a fourth in medicine. Then he offered his services to the Paris Society.

Schweitzer held some theological views which were unpopular at the time. Because of this, the Society nearly turned him down, and finally accepted him

HENRY A. RODGERS is professor of Greek and Bible at Grove City College, Grove City, Pa.

only on condition that he would not preach. In 1913, with his wife, a nurse, he set out for Africa. At Lambaréné he built a hospital from the ground up. By 1914 he had more practice than he could handle. For over forty years he gave himself in this work as a true and loyal servant of Jesus Christ.

Reaction to Liberalism

In this chapter on Albert Schweitzer we are primarily interested in his contribution to religious thought, and must therefore bypass the fascinating story of his medical work in Africa.

He was primarily a New Testament scholar; and his major work in New Testament study was a re-action against the liberal school of German theology of his day. The principal goal of these liberals was to study Jesus with modern methods, and so make him intelligible to the modern mind. They tried to re-discover "the historical Jesus" as a man who had lived in a certain period of history, under certain political and social conditions, and had proclaimed his universal message. Above all, they wanted to be strictly scientific, by which they meant eliminating everything that might be attributed to superstition, like the miracles, or Jesus' supernatural relationship with God. Such things, they explained, belonged to the thinking of those who wrote down Jesus' teach-ings in the Gospels, and not to Jesus himself. Jesus was thought of as the great Teacher, and the "king-dom of God" would come when all men fully under-stood and obeyed his teachings.

Among the "superstitious" parts of the New Testa-ment that the liberals rejected were the many references to the Second Coming of Christ, the Last Judgment, the end of the world, heaven, and hell. These are known to theologians as eschatology, the doctrine of the Last Things. That these loom large in the Gospel records, and even in the recorded sayings of Jesus, no one has ever doubted. But Schweitzer became convinced that they should not be eliminated from the teachings of Jesus—on the contrary, Jesus as a man who had lived in the generation that believed in these things had actually believed in them himself.

In his book *The Mystery of the Kingdom of God,* Schweitzer deals with three mysteries, which he believes were in the mind of Jesus and which seem to explain all the eschatological sayings of Jesus. The first, the mystery of the kingdom of God, Schweitzer finds in Matthew 10:23 where Jesus tells the twelve apostles, as he sends them out to preach, "Verily I say unto you, ye shall not have gone over the cities of Israel, till the Son of man be come." [1] From this and other passages, Schweitzer decided that Jesus actually expected the Kingdom to appear in a supernatural way at that particular time, and that he was disappointed when it failed.

The second, the mystery of the Messiahship, is based on the coincidence of the phrase "who is to come" in Matthew 11:3 and 14. From this Schweitzer concluded that people thought of Jesus—not of John the Baptist—as Elijah, who was to prepare the way for the coming of Christ. Only Jesus, he insists, at that time realized that when the Son of Man should come on the clouds of heaven, it would be himself.

The third mystery, that of the Passion, is, according to Schweitzer, the most important of all. Having been disappointed about the coming of the Son of Man, that is, himself, at the time he sent out the Twelve, Jesus came to the conclusion, from Isaiah 53, that as Messiah he must first die for his people. So he

[1] King James Version (KJV).

foretold his death, then deliberately went to Jerusalem and provoked the authorities to crucify him, expecting in that way to bring about his own Second Coming and the kingdom of God.

Facing Fresh Questions

Schweitzer believed that he had solved the difficulties he had found in the liberal interpretation of the historical Jesus. But his solution raises as many problems as it solves. One of these is the purpose of Jesus' teachings. If he was primarily concerned with establishing a supernatural, perfect Kingdom, why should he bother to give ethical instructions like the Sermon on the Mount? Schweitzer recognized this problem and gave his answer: Such teachings were intended to show his immediate followers what they could do as works of repentance in order that the Kingdom might come. They would not be needed after the Kingdom had come, for then sin would be done away with, and those who shared in the Kingdom would naturally do the right thing. In this sense, he calls the teachings of Jesus "interim ethics," for the time being, until the Kingdom should come. (Of course, since the Kingdom has not yet come in the eschatological sense, they are still valid today.) For to Schweitzer, Jesus was not primarily a Teacher, but a Redeemer, the Christ who will be king.

This insight also answers another problem raised by Schweitzer's interpretation: that of Jesus' alleged mistakes. In connection with the mystery of the kingdom of God, Schweitzer believes that Jesus had expected the Kingdom to come at the time he sent out the twelve apostles to preach and had been disappointed and upset at its failure to materialize. Then he had come to the conclusion that he must force it to come by dying to redeem his people. This was the mystery of the Passion. If Schweitzer is right, Jesus was mistaken on both counts. The Kingdom did not appear when the twelve went out to preach, and it did not come immediately following his death. And if Jesus was mistaken about two of the "mysteries," how can we be sure he was not mistaken about the third, that of his Messiahship, that is, his certainty that he himself would be revealed as the Christ when the Kingdom should come?

Schweitzer does not answer this question in just this form, but he does deal with the basic problem in the concluding chapter of *The Quest of the Historical Jesus*.[2] To those who would claim that he has destroyed faith in Jesus, he replies that the Jesus he destroyed never really existed except in the inventive minds of the liberal theologians. He claims to have loosed Jesus from the fetters of this false interpretation and restored him to his rightful place as the great King. He even quotes with approval Paul's dictum in II Corinthians, 5:16: "Though we have known Christ after the flesh, yet now henceforth we know him no more." [3] That is, his faith is not in Jesus the man, understood in human terms, but in Christ the Son of God, whom we know by his spirit in our hearts, and to whom our response must be not in our minds, but in our wills, as we obey him.

Schweitzer was well aware that some of the liberal theologians would refuse to accept his eschatological interpretations of Jesus. He made them come to grips with the problem, however, and so he was partially responsible for the method of Bible study called Form Criticism. These scholars who questioned whether Jesus had eschatological ideas were forced to attribute more and more of his sayings to the writers

[2] New York: The Macmillan Company, 1948.
[3] KJV.

of the Gospels, or to the tradition from which they got their information. This in turn led to the study of the tradition itself, and became what is known as Form Criticism. This movement has produced some very learned works by such scholars as Martin Dibelius, Rudolf Bultmann, and others.

Today, largely because of Schweitzer's pioneering work, no reputable theologian can ignore the eschatological element in the Gospels. C. H. Dodd, of Cambridge, has interpreted this teaching as what he calls "realized eschatology." He points out that Jesus spoke of the Kingdom as not always future, but in some sense present. "The kingdom of God is in the midst of you." [4] Dodd therefore seeks to show that Jesus used eschatological language because it was the natural mode of expression in his day, but that he meant by it something much more universal than his contemporaries understood.

Basis for Humanitarian Work

Thus Schweitzer has affected modern Protestant thought. But he will be remembered rather as the great humanitarian, who gave up theology and philosophy to demonstrate the love of God by his medical mission to the neglected people of Africa. In the last analysis, this is simply the practical expression of his faith.

It arises first from his sense of dedicated stewardship. In his *Memoirs of Childhood and Youth*,[5] he recalls winning a schoolboy fight, only to have the elation of victory snatched away by the loser's remark, "If I had broth every day as you do, I could beat you." From that day on, Schweitzer always believed that God gave him exceptional powers of body

[4] Luke 17:21, Revised Standard Version (RSV).
[5] New York: The Macmillan Company, 1949.

and mind for some special service to mankind. He was trying to perform that service at Lambaréné.

It arises also from the cardinal principle of his *Philosophy of Civilization*,[6] which is "Reverence for Life." His critics have charged that his reverence for all forms of animal life, even insects, is based on Hindu pantheism. The resemblance is coincidental. To Schweitzer, needlessly to kill another living creature, which wills to live as he wills to live, is to transgress the purpose of God in creating it. It is therefore a Christian motive.

But his devotion to his work was, more than all else, simply the expression of his obedience to the royal Christ, to whom he unconditionally surrendered his will. As he says in the closing chapter of *The Quest of the Historical Jesus,* faith is a matter of the will, more than of the understanding. This is the basic faith by which he lived; and it is capable of commanding a devotion and self-sacrifice such as the "historical Jesus" could not call forth. On this faith let Albert Schweitzer be judged. As his Master said, "You shall know them by their fruits."

FOR FURTHER READING

Albert Schweitzer, *Out of My Life and Thought* (New York: Henry Holt and Company, Incorporated, 1949; also New American Library paperback edition). An autobiography.

———, *The Quest of the Historical Jesus* (New York: The Macmillan Company, 1948).

———, *The Mystery of the Kingdom of God* (New York: The Macmillan Company, 1950).

6 New York: The Macmillan Company, 1949.

II

Walter Rauschenbusch

BY ROBERT T. HANDY

For about a decade, Walter Rauschenbusch was one of the best-known ministers in America. He became a national figure suddenly and unexpectedly in 1907. From then until his death in 1918, Rauschenbusch was greatly in demand as preacher, lecturer, and writer. Five important books and a number of smaller pieces came from his pen in those years. He was regarded as the central figure in the movement known as the "social gospel," which was then very influential in American Protestantism. Henry Van Dusen has classed him with Jonathan Edwards and Horace Bushnell as one of the three most influential men in the thought of the American church.

Walter Rauschenbusch was born in 1861 in Rochester, New York. His German-born father came to this country as a missionary in the middle of the last century, and soon thereafter left Lutheranism to enter the Baptist fold. Young Walter was educated in both Germany and America, and graduated from the Rochester Theological Seminary in 1886. He desired "to preach and save souls." In order to do

ROBERT T. HANDY is professor of church history at Union Theological Seminary, New York, N. Y.

this, he felt he must live literally by the teachings and spirit of Jesus.

It was with this spirit of commitment that he accepted the pastorate of the Second German Baptist Church in New York's tough West Side, not far from the region popularly known as Hell's Kitchen. His was a congregation of working people, and the earnest young pastor soon became acutely aware of their difficult struggles against poverty and disease, especially in hard times. Their suffering forced him to confront social problems. As he put it, his social view "did not come from the church. It came from outside. It came through personal contact with poverty, and when I saw how men toiled all their life long, hard, toilsome lives, and at the end had almost nothing to show for it; how strong men begged for work and could not get it in hard times; how little children died—oh, the children's funerals! they gripped my heart—that was one of the things I always went away thinking about—why did the children have to die?" (From an address in 1913.) Actually he suffered with his people—leaving his bed too early after an influenza attack in order to minister to sick and needy parishioners, the illness recurred and left him deaf. But this did not hinder his desire to improve social conditions.

Committed Christian that he was, he could not keep his social thinking separate from his religious thinking; and so he sought to bring the two together. He read widely in social and economic literature, but also in the writings of men who were advocating concern for social issues from a distinctively Christian point of view. This was the distinctive thing about him—the effort to emphasize both evangelical faith and social reconstruction. It was then an unfamiliar combination.

A deeply thoughtful analysis of Rauschenbusch by Winthrop S. Hudson is aptly entitled "A Lonely Prophet." He was lonely not only because his deafness served to isolate him somewhat from those around him but also because this fundamental aim— to combine the *religious* and the *social* passion—was so often misunderstood. Some could not believe he had the first because he had the second also; others seized upon the second but remained oblivious to the first. Yet the key to understanding him is to see that his lifework was precisely the effort to keep both emphases, with priority always on the first.

His Understanding of the Kingdom of God

The seminary from which he had graduated had not forgotten its able son, and in 1897 Rauschenbusch returned to Rochester to teach, finally settling into the chair of church history. But it was to be not as a church historian but as a social prophet that Rauschenbusch became famous. He wrote a book to discharge a debt to his former parishioners, to help ease the pressure that bore them down. *Christianity and the Social Crisis* appeared in that year of financial panic, 1907.

His thesis was that "the essential purpose of Christianity was to transform human society into the kingdom of God by regenerating all human relations and reconstituting them in accordance with the will of God," but that this purpose had been obscured through the centuries and now had to be recovered. Coming at a time when the social questions were among the most popular issues of the day, the book won instant acclaim and set its author at the forefront of the growing number of pastors and laymen anxious to deal with social concerns from a Christian viewpoint. Rauschenbusch became the leader of the social gospel movement, a career interrupted by his death of cancer in 1918.

Rauschenbusch was especially concerned to elaborate on the full meaning of the kingdom of God, and he kept both his tongue and pen busy at this task throughout his lifetime. He wrote: *Prayers of the Social Awakening* (1910), *Christianizing the Social Order* (1912), *The Social Principles of Jesus* (1916), and *A Theology for the Social Gospel* (1917).

The concept of the kingdom of God was for him a profoundly religious concept which was central in the teachings of Jesus and which included the entire life of man and society. As he said in the concluding chapter of the book that deals most with social and economic problems:

"This is a religious book from beginning to end. Its sole concern is for the kingdom of God and the salvation of men. But the kingdom of God includes the economic life; for it means the progressive transformation of all human affairs by the thought and spirit of Christ." [1]

He warned against substituting social activities for religious; he insisted that not less religion but more— of the right kind—was needed.

For Rauschenbusch, the kingdom of God was not an earthly utopia that men could create. He emphasized that it was divine in its origin, progress, and consummation. It was for him the revelation of the power, the righteousness, and the love of God. He knew it as both a present reality among men and a future hope to be fully disclosed only in the fullness

[1] From *Christianizing the Social Order,* by Walter Rauschenbusch. Copyright 1912, by The Macmillan Company, New York. Used by permission.

of time. He did believe that it was progressively being realized:

"A progressive Kingdom of righteousness happens all the time in installments, like our own sanctification. Our race will come to an end in due time; the astronomical clock is already ticking which will ring in the end. Meanwhile we are on the march toward the kingdom of God, and getting our reward by every fractional realization of it which makes us hungry for more." [2]

He summoned men and women to serve the Kingdom in their lives:

"Every human life is so placed that it can share with God in the creation of the Kingdom, or can resist and retard its progress. The Kingdom is for each of us the supreme task and the supreme gift of God. By accepting it as a task, we experience it as a gift. By laboring for it we enter into the joy and peace of the Kingdom as our divine fatherland and habitation." [3]

The lives of many Christians were shaped by their response to the call to serve in the Kingdom task.

His Contribution

As the man who was the most conspicuous representative of the social gospel, Walter Rauschenbusch made an important and permanent contribution to American Christian thought. He and those like him pointed out in an unforgettable way the social dimension of life and the social aspects of the gospel of Christ.

To be sure, he was the child of his time, and most

[2] From *A Theology for the Social Gospel.* Copyright 1917, by The Macmillan Company, New York. Used by permission.
[3] *Ibid.*

of us would find ourselves quite out of sympathy with some of his statements. In explaining what Jesus' idea of the Kingdom was, he no doubt read in too much of his own progressive and evolutionary view, and did not give proper weight to the eschatological aspect. Strong for the Kingdom, he probably did not value highly enough the role of the church. In stressing the immanence of God, in identifying him so closely with humanity, Rauschenbusch minimized the transcendence, the majesty, and the sovereignty of God. In defining sin as essentially selfishness he did less than justice to the classic Christian understanding of sin as pride. As for his social views, a case can be made that they lacked the sturdy quality and real insight of his religious thought. They reflected the mild progressive radicalism of the type that had considerable vogue before World War I; though he was not a socialist, his analysis of the social order drew on socialist thought. And clearly he overestimated the degree to which the nation and its institutions had become Christianized.

His contribution, therefore, was set in a framework that clearly bears the stamp of an age that has passed. Yet it is impressive to observe how he avoided the pitfalls into which the later social gospel slipped. Though he was influenced by the optimism of his time, he also understood the tragic character of life and warned that men and nations might take the wrong road. Although some of his followers in their social passion neglected personal religion, Rauschenbusch himself never did and, had his followers listened to his full message, they would not have neglected it either. He never confused social reconstruction, necessary as he believed it to be, with the experience of salvation, which he sought to enrich and expand by bringing it into proper relation to the kingdom of God.

FOR FURTHER READING

D. R. Sharpe, *Walter Rauschenbusch* (New York: The Macmillan Company, 1942). A book about Rauschenbusch, now out of print. Available in libraries.

Benjamin E. Mays, ed., *A Gospel for the Social Awakening: Selections from the Writings of Walter Rauschenbusch* (New York: Association Press, 1950).

Benson Y. Landis, ed., *A Rauschenbusch Reader* (New York: Harper & Brothers, 1957).

III

Sören Kierkegaard

BY FRED J. DENBEAUX

Sören Kierkegaard would not be comfortable with the nervously cautious thinkers of our age. He not only was indifferent to public opinion but he attacked all those who relied upon the support of the masses. For Kierkegaard, the truth, the costly and painful truth, constitutes the only standard of the right. The question of truth before every man is the question of whether he will dare to pay the cost.

Kierkegaard was born in Denmark in 1813 and, except for a few brief visits to Berlin, lived out his life in his homeland. He was very close to his father who, in spite of the fact that he was a practical man, communicated to his son a deeply serious concern for the problems of Christian life and thought. After the completion of his work at the university and after some years of indecision, Kierkegaard began to prepare himself for a church parish. Because of a number of factors, not the least of which was his need for personal freedom, he was unable to become a clergyman. Similarly he fell in love and planned for mar-

FRED J. DENBEAUX is chairman of the Bible department at Wellesley College, Wellesley, Mass., and a Presbyterian minister.

riage, but for many reasons, including that of temperament, he was unable to marry. Occupied with neither a vocation nor a family and supported by a fairly substantial inheritance from his father, he was able to produce an incredibly large amount of literature. For this we have reason to be grateful, since his thinking has added a measure of depth to the thought of many contemporary Protestants, Jews, and Roman Catholics.

The Creature Thinking About God

Let us examine the thought of this man who has come to be one of the major influences on Protestant theology in this century.

Kierkegaard has no interest in the traditional arguments for the existence of God. Whatever is ultimate and meaningful can never be proved. God is never an object, not even a divine object. He is either the Absolute, by which *we* are proved, or he is nothing.

In either case, God is not contained within our system of logic. Thus, in a very important passage, Kierkegaard says, "So also with the proof for God's existence. As long as I keep my hold on the proof, i.e., continue to demonstrate, the existence does not come out, if for no other reason than that I am engaged in proving it; but when I let the proof go, the existence is there." Here Kierkegaard reflects the biblical notion that *faithful obedience* rather than thought describes man's relationship to God. Whenever I try to prove that God exists, I actually lose my relationship to him, since proving moves me from the role of a servant to that of a lawyer.

Kierkegaard also believes that we cannot come to God through thought because we can never leave the *structure* in which we exist as *creatures*. Any thought about God always, if it be true thought, carries with

it the understanding of both the relationship between
God and man and the difference between the Creator
and the creature. Kierkegaard says that God is "the
limit to which the reason repeatedly comes." Thus
one of the surest indications that there is a God is
found in the fact that we have difficulty "thinking"
God. Our mind cannot produce the images that will
sustain a true knowledge of God. We can produce as
many arguments for him as against him. Thinking
cannot produce . . . God. Our mind is shattered by
God in the sense that one must say that he believes
in God not because his mind has found God but
because it has failed to find him. Only as one is
sensitive to the *limit* can one be sure that one is
responding as a creature must to his Creator.

Thus Kierkegaard reintroduces the biblical and
Reformed notion that we shall think about God as a
creature or we shall not think about him at all.

How Can We Understand Christ?

We can best understand Kierkegaard's contribution if we remember that he defended the orthodox
view of Jesus in quite unorthodox language. He accepted the traditional and trinitarian view of Jesus
Christ. What he was trying to do was to create a new
approach to our ancient faith.

Again, as Kierkegaard sees it, our approach to
Jesus Christ is through a *relationship* and not through
speculation. This means that Christ is not a problem
in doctrine. One cannot get to Christ through correct
thinking. Christ is understood only through his Lordship over our lives. Or, to put it the other way
around, we can understand Christ, not through ideas,
but through discipleship.

We begin, then, by understanding that Christ is
Lord, not because of what he teaches but because of

what he does. He brings to men not only the assurance of God's love but also the possibility of being participants in that love, through receiving the grace of God's forgiveness. All of Kierkegaard's art, at this point, is calculated to evoke a response from his readers. He does not so much instruct us on his view of Christ as he tries to have us respond and, out of our response, to understand. This means that we must, as we think through the whole problem of Jesus Christ, be sure that we do not get lost in the externals of discussion. Christ is not Lord to us because of the authority of the church or because he did miracles in an astounding and interesting manner. He is our Lord because we are his disciples or he is not Lord at all.

A characteristic phrase of Kierkegaard's is "the solitary individual." No one has stressed the importance of individual decision (and of individuality) more than he, for we do not become disciples in a crowd. We become disciples only as individuals. We become disciples not because others have believed but in spite of it. We become disciples of Christ not because the world supports us, but because it does not. Every Christian must first approach Christ in this manner, without proof, without support, and in utter faith.

The Offense of Faith

Faith, however, is not easy. It is certainly not an act of blindness, for God in his wisdom makes it impossible to accept Christ easily. Kierkegaard points out over and over again that Christ comes to us in a form that insults both our notion of self-reliance and our intelligence. He makes much of the saying of Jesus, "Blessed is he who takes no offense at me." It is inevitable either that we shall be offended or that we shall believe.

What is the offense of faith? It can take many forms. We would welcome a God of light, but he comes to us crucified. We would welcome a God with whom we could be happy, and instead we are confronted with him whom we have slain. We are offended because we can never come before God neutrally but always in guilt. We are offended because the Christ who comes does not come in the form that we expect. We would be happier if he came as a god of war, so that we could join our sword to his in the battle against unrighteousness (always conveniently with the enemy and never with ourselves). But the Christ does not come with a sword, and he asks us to put our sword away; so we are offended.

Therefore, Christ is always the occasion of either offense or faith. He is the one either before whom we stumble and fall on our knees or else from whom we turn in defensive pride. He is our Saviour, but we shall never know him as such if we become offended, because it is from ourselves that he saves us.

How Can We Understand Ourselves?

What makes man human? Although Kierkegaard does not emphasize the word, he thinks of man in terms of his *creatureliness*.

Man's creatureliness lies in the fact that he stands between life and death. Made in the image of God, he knows what it means to feel the presence of eternity. Feeling the nearness of eternity, utterly dependent upon it for his meaning, he also knows that he dies, and that he cannot escape death. These two factors constitute both his problem and his possibility for immortality, creates his anguish or his *nervous humanness*.

Man sins in that he is unwilling to live in faith and therefore to be nervously human. He prefers to live either with life or with death but not with both. He seeks to escape creatureliness either by pretending that he will not die or by assuming that there is no eternity.

He refuses to bear uncertainty and anguish. Either he turns his back on death by pretending that immortality is automatically a part of all life or he tries to forget his anguish by becoming an animal.

It is precisely this anguish, this willingness to live neither as an animal (unaware of eternity) nor as an angel (indifferent to death), which marks the humanness from which we fall when we sin. It is also this humanness, this willingness to risk death as we trust God, which signals the beginning of our redemption. Thus the Christ of love returns us to our creatureliness by saving us from the need of false securities. The Lord Christ, by accepting death even while he trusted in God, restores meaning to creaturely existence. By faith man dares to become what without faith he was afraid to be—a human being.

FOR FURTHER READING

Sören Kierkegaard, *Purity of Heart* (New York: Harper & Brothers, 1956). Introduction by Douglas V. Steere. This is the best book to begin with for an understanding of Kierkegaard's philosophy.

Robert Bretall, ed., *A Kierkegaard Anthology* (Princeton, N. J.: Princeton University Press, 1946). Read selections in this book, then decide where you want to go next.

David E. Roberts, *Existentialism and Religious Belief* (New York: Oxford University Press, 1957). Read this book for an introduction and understanding of existentialism. It contains a good section on Kierkegaard.

IV

Karl Barth

BY THOMAS F. TORRANCE

Karl Barth is incontestably the greatest figure in modern theology since Schleiermacher, occupying an honored position among the great elite of the church —Augustine, Anselm, Aquinas, Luther, and Calvin.

Karl Barth, born in 1886, began his career as a minister in Geneva, and then continued it in Safenwil, in Aargau Canton. It was there he published the first edition of his celebrated commentary on the Epistle to the Romans [1] (1918), which exploded like a bomb in the religious thought of Europe, and marked the beginning of one of the great eras in the history of Christian thought. Two years later he was called to a chair at the University of Göttingen in Germany. In 1925 he went to the University of Münster, and in 1930 he became professor at the University of Bonn, where he lectured to overflowing

THOMAS F. TORRANCE is professor of Christian dogmatics at the University of Edinburgh, Scotland, and outstanding interpreter of Barth to the English-speaking world.

[1] Karl Barth, ed., Bible. Epistle to the Romans. Translated from the 6th edition by E. C. Hoskyns (London: Oxford University Press, 1933).

classrooms until forced to leave under the Nazi regime because he refused to take the oath demanded by Hitler. Called back to Basel in Switzerland, his home, he has remained there ever since.

How Barth's Thought Developed

Three distinct stages mark the development of Barth's thought. In them he wrestled with modern philosophy and then came out with the consistent biblical dogmatics of which he is the master exponent.

I

In his early period Karl Barth's theology falls within the thought forms represented by Schleiermacher—that is, the liberal theology of religious individualism that developed in the nineteenth century. But Barth's liberalism and idealism were of a strange sort, for even at this period we find searching questions directed to everything before him as the young theologian sought to probe down to the depths. But this ruthless criticism was mainly in the form of self-criticism, for Barth was acutely aware of sin as man's desire to be independent of God. Out of this stage came his commentary on the Epistle to the Romans (1918).

II

The second stage was marked by a radical rewriting of that book. The first edition had not received much notice, but the second edition raised a storm in the theological and philosophical thought of Germany and Switzerland. In it Barth expressed his deep dissatisfaction with the subjectivism of Protestant theology which confounded man with God and put man in the place of God. The new edition was deliberately intended to create an upheaval, and it succeeded.

This is the stage of Barth's thought in which he comes under the influence of Kierkegaard, and his searching questions begin to bear some positive fruit. The main theme can be described thus: Let God be God, and let man learn again how to be man, instead of trying to be as God. The supreme sin of man is that even in his religion he is always twisting the truth to suit his own selfish ends and private ideas. Barth is here revealed to be a real genius in theological penetration and expression, for with the most powerful and dramatic strokes of his pen that analysis was driven into all aspects of modern life and thought. His *Romans* translation shattered the selfish individualism of theological liberalism or else made it hysterically angry! But its whole purpose was to make room again for the holy and transcendent God of the Bible.

When man is thus confronted by God, there there is collision, crucifixion. The cross is seen to be the supreme and unique event of the meeting between Holy God and sinful man, and at the cross all the subtle attempts of man at self-deification and self-aggrandizement are exposed. That is particularly true of religious man, for it is primarily religious man who is the sinner. It was, after all, religious man who crucified Jesus! And yet the incredible, breathtaking fact about the cross is the sheer grace and infinite love of God, which tears away from man his rags of self-deceit, and clothes him in the righteousness of God in order to stand him on his feet again as a child of the Heavenly Father.

This is the stage in which Barth's theology is *dialectical* in form. His searching questions have led him to the point where he thinks about the contrasts of Holy God and sinful man, Creator and creature, grace and judgment, God's *Yes* and yet God's *No*. And here Barth is faced with a fundamental problem of all theology and all thinking about God. It is *man* who thinks, *man* who asks searching questions about God, *man* who is hungry to know God, to speak about him and make judgments about him. But when that man stands face to face with God, he discovers that he stands at the bar of God's judgment and it is *God* who speaks to him. *What is important is not what man thinks about God but what God thinks about man!*

This is also the stage when Barth thinks of the relation between God and man in terms of continuing crisis, in which eternity confronts time and God is always invading history and becoming contemporaneous. All meeting with God is thought of as recurring encounter between the divine "Thou" and the human "I." This was Barth's way of answering the problem of communication: how we are to get across to Jesus or let Jesus Christ get across to us without secretly turning him into a twentieth-century figure who is only too harmless and familiar.

The solution for Barth came as a result of tireless criticism of himself and a relentless searching of the Scripture. He let Christ speak to him out of the Bible not as one who could confirm or agree with the theologian's answers but as one who was *against* Barth's own self and against man's desire to make out of Jesus a modern idol.

From now on his theology became the *theology of the Word*. Henceforth the concrete Word of God, speaking to him out of the Holy Scriptures, becomes the object of theological knowledge and security.

III

In the second stage Barth had written the first volume of a new dogmatics, called *Christian Dogmatics*. Now, in his determination to lay the foundations for a consistent and thoroughgoing biblical theology, he found he had to rewrite the whole thing. In the first volume of *Church Dogmatics* (1932), he swept aside all the language of idealist philosophy, all the language of Kierkegaard and the existentialist misunderstanding of Kierkegaard; he threw out the old dialectic between eternity and time and its language of timeless crisis, and interpreted the Word of God in the most concrete terms, strictly in the terms of the Person of Jesus Christ, the Word made flesh, who is true God and true man in one Person.

His Contribution

Barth's arrival at this understanding of Christ is the decisive point in his theological development. We can therefore now turn from tracing his development to describing three of his major contributions to Christian thinking.

The Centrality of Jesus Christ. The great heart of Barth's theology is the doctrine of Jesus Christ. In him who is true God and true man in one person we are confronted with a mystery that is more to be adored than expressed, so that even when we have done all that it is our duty to do in theological understanding and expression, we must confess that we are unprofitable servants of the Word of God, whose efforts fall far short of its incarnate glory. Nevertheless, we must give ourselves to the obedience of Christ, and let all our thinking be taken captive by him. It is only as we become conformable in mind to Christ that we can formulate aright our doctrine of God—Father, Son, and Holy Spirit. That is why the doctrine of the person and work of Christ forms the center and core of all Christian theology and determines all our thinking in the Christian church. And that is why everything depends on faithful obedience to the Scriptures.

It is in this way that Barth himself has already given the church a most valuable account of Christology. For more than a hundred years the theologians and scholars of Europe and America have been seeking to express as fully as possible the truth about Jesus Christ. The documents of the New Testament have been subjected to the most elaborate research the world has ever given them, and how many and how baffling are the problems they have revealed! But in Karl Barth we have another Athanasius, doing battle against misunderstanding on the right and on the left, and out of it all leading the Christian church back to a fuller and far more adequate account of the person and work of Christ than we have known for centuries.

The Doctrine of the Church. Karl Barth's theology has become an ecumenical force not only because it strikes down into the heart of the matter as it affects every church and because it brings within its range the whole history of catholic theology, but also because it has raised into the forefront in unparalleled fashion the doctrine of the church. That was not his deliberate intention. His intention has always been to clear away the ground and to confront the church with Jesus Christ in all his majesty and grace. But in doing this he has forced upon our generation a reconsideration of the doctrine of the church as the body of Christ, and a reconsideration of the whole procedure of theology as the discipline that we must undertake within the bounds of the church where the voice of Christ is heard in the preaching of the gospel and where Christ makes us able to participate in his life, death, and resurrection by his Spirit through Word and sacraments.

In this Karl Barth follows above all in the tradition of John Calvin, though he has brought his searching questions to bear on the teaching of Calvin as well, with great benefit in a remarkable clarification of the doctrine of election.

The New Creature in Christ. In some ways the most characteristic aspect of Barth's theology is his emphasis upon the new humanity in Jesus Christ, incarnate, crucified, and risen, and who will come again to renew the heaven and the earth. This is particularly characteristic, because here Barth's thought moves, as elsewhere, in what he calls a "third dimension." By that he means that whereas many theologians in Europe and America think primarily in terms of two dimensions, God and man, eternity and time, Barth's thinking is governed by the dimension of the union of God and man in Christ. Thus he thinks not in terms of man but in terms of the new humanity that mankind has in Jesus Christ risen from the dead. That is Barth's Christian humanism, and it is that which lies behind his consuming interest in the everyday affairs of our human life and work, social and political as well as religious. (This interest is seen best in his essays published under the title *Against the Stream,* noted under "For Further Reading.")

The central issue here is in many ways the doctrine of the resurrection of Jesus Christ in body. If Jesus Christ is risen only in spirit—whatever that means!— then he is, so to speak, but a ghost with no relevance to men and women of flesh and blood in history. If Jesus Christ exists no longer as man, only at the right hand of the Father, then we have little ground for hope in this life. It is the risen humanity of Christ that forms the very center of the Christian's hope, for this is the ground and basis of the Christian's own renewal of all creation. The Christian church that believes in the resurrection of Jesus Christ from the dead has no right to despair of "this weary world of ours" or to be afraid of its utter dissolution into nothing. Jesus Christ is risen from the dead and completely victorious over all the mighty demonic forces of destruction that threaten our world. In him we can lift up our heads and laugh in face of fear and disaster, for in him we are more than conquerors over all, knowing that God, who raised up Jesus Christ from the dead, wearing our humanity, will not suffer the world for which Christ died and rose to see corruption.

The doctrine of the new humanity in Christ is the new wine that bursts the old bottles. It is because the Christian church participates already through the Spirit in the risen Jesus that the Christian church must refuse to live in the graveclothes of the past; it must ever be seeking to work out in the present the appropriate forms of its new life in Christ. That is the realism that lies behind the evangelization of the world and the Christian insistence that from day to day in every sphere of our world we must live out the new life which we are given by the Saviour of men.

FOR FURTHER READING

Karl Barth, *Dogmatics in Outline* (Philosophical Library, 1949). Read this book to see Barth's comprehensive theology in brief scope.

————, *Prayer* (Philadelphia: Westminster Press, 1952).

————, *Against the Stream* (Philosophical Library, 1954). These two books are brief and readable on certain subjects.

————, *The Humanity of God* (John Knox Press, 1960).

Georges Casalis, *Portrait of Karl Barth* (Doubleday and Co., 1963).

V

Reinhold Niebuhr

BY CLAUDE WELCH

"Moral man and immoral society"—this striking phrase is the title of a book published in 1932 by a man whose name has become a household word in American Protestantism—Reinhold Niebuhr. This was a striking book, even shocking to some, for in it Niebuhr laid siege to many of the most confidently held dogmas of the early twentieth century. Looking back, we can see that *Moral Man and Immoral Society* [1] not only brought its author into prominence, but also was the sign and foretaste of profound change in the mood and pattern of Protestant thinking in the United States.

The spirit of America in the 1920's was one of confidence and optimism. Even World War I and the early years of the great depression had not shaken the conviction that our social problems were approaching solution. This temper found expression in the churches in the movement called the "social

CLAUDE WELCH teaches at the University of Pennsylvania.

[1] New York: Charles Scribner's Sons, 1932.

gospel." Many of the leaders were sure that all of men's social relations were in fact being brought progressively under the law of Christ.

In *Moral Man and Immoral Society,* Reinhold Niebuhr erupted in violent protest against these easy assumptions. Analyzing the problems of individual and social morality, he saw that the beliefs in inevitable progress through growing goodwill and social education were illusions, both dangerous and contrary to the gospel. What can be achieved in individual righteousness may be quite impossible for society. Social decisions are never so clear-cut as decisions about personal morality; they are always, to use a favorite word of Niebuhr, ambiguous. We never have a clean choice between pure truth and pure error, good and evil. In man-to-man relationships, in small groups, we can often achieve a high level of morality, of unselfish love; but in large societies, in the conflicts between groups in society, the moral problem is different. Relations are impersonal; men are not related to each other in face-to-face contact, but as representatives of groups with interests to be served. There is not only the self-centeredness of individuals, but there is also the egoism of races, of corporations, and of nations. And this egoism is not restrained and checked by conscience and good will and reasonableness, for our social responsibilities are confused, and our reasoning is unwittingly distorted by the interests of the groups to which we belong.

Thus, Niebuhr comments, "individuals are never as immoral as the social situations in which they are involved and which they symbolize." There is an impersonal and brutal character about the behavior of all human "collectives," with their self-interest and group egoism, which makes social conflict inevitable. Appeals to conscience, efforts of moral persuasion, which may be quite effective in man-to-man relationships, are simply inadequate to resolve social conflict. "Love" is not sufficient for the restraint of evil. Unselfishness is properly the highest ideal for individuals, but the highest moral ideal for society seems to be justice, maintained even by force. Hence the paradox: moral man—immoral society.

A Detroit Pastor

The vigor of Reinhold Niebuhr's challenge to complacency and optimism did not come from mere academic interest in another theory of human conduct. Much came from the experience of a pastor who was confronted in the lives of his congregation with the brutal realities of social distress. Born in Missouri in 1892, he studied at Elmhurst College, Eden Theological Seminary, and Yale University. In 1915 he became pastor of the Bethel Evangelical Church in Detroit, ministering to a congregation of workers in the automobile industry. Here the theme later to be developed in *Moral Man and Immoral Society* was learned in pastoral experience. He describes this ministry in an autobiographical essay in the book *Reinhold Niebuhr: His Religious, Social, and Political Thought.*[2]

In 1928 he left Detroit to teach in the field of social ethics at Union Theological Seminary, New York City, where he taught for many years.

We have seen how Niebuhr was sharply critical of the optimism of the 1920's (especially among the religious and idealistic) regarding social progress. He was not rejecting the moral earnestness, or the demand of the social gospel that all life, including social structures, he brought under the reign of Christ. Far

[2] Edited by Charles W. Kegley and Robert W. Bretall (New York: The Macmillan Company, 1956).

from it! Rather, he was puncturing the illusions and the self-deceptions that nullified effective social action. He was calling for a realistic recognition of the depth and complexity of social evil, and of the possibilities for effective transformation, thus for an adequate strategy of attack.

As Niebuhr sees the problem, the Christian is always in a paradoxical position. He must face without flinching the reality and complexity of social evil. Yet "realism" is not enough. Meaning for life has to be gained from insight into a principle or ideal that lies outside the situation. We must always insist on the relevance of the Christian ethical ideal to just these social situations—to industrial Detroit, to international relations, to race and class conflicts. The Christian is bound by the law of love, though the law of love can never be purely embodied in social life.

The "Impossible Possibility"

This problem has been even more sharply defined in *An Interpretation of Christian Ethics,*[3] in which Niebuhr speaks of love as the "impossible possibility" and of "the relevance of an impossible ethical ideal." The Christian must act in the light of both the law of love and the genuine possibilities for action. There is no society in which the law of love can work perfectly; yet the law of love provides our motive and standard for action. Only in the light of the law of love can sin be seen for what it is, and only in this light can relative achievements of justice be judged.

The Christian cannot despair or become complacent, lying down in the face of tyranny and social injustice. Nor can he deceive himself with the illusion that some program or other will provide a permanent solution to men's problems. Every action, every social

[3] New York: Harper & Brothers, 1935.

program, will be a compromise. It will be only an approximation of justice, a choice between available alternatives in the light of the law of love.

From this understanding of our ethical situation, we can turn to two other themes that have been of great interest to Niebuhr: the meaning of history, and the nature of man and his sin.

The Meaning of History

Niebuhr has discussed at length the meaning of history in the second volume of *The Nature and Destiny of Man,* in *Faith and History, The Irony of American History,* and in *The Self and the Dramas of History.*[4] The meaning of history is revealed in Christ. He is the "center" of history, the disclosure of God's rule in history, and the meaning of God's love. In him God reveals his law of love and manifests his power to be gracious to men. In Christ new resources of love, wisdom, and power are made available to men. Yet life in history is never fulfilled. Christ comes in judgment as well as in promise. No social order or proposal for reform can be simply identified with the will of God. No human achievement is ever free from the limitations of human finitude or the temptations of self-justification and rationalism. Every idealism and scheme for the solution of humanity's ills is subject to transformation into an instrument of power over others. Much indeed may be achieved, but every creative achievement brings new possibilities of injustice.

Therefore, history always awaits fulfillment in the kingdom of God, which stands "beyond history." The Kingdom is disclosed in Christ, and he is the judge. In him the law is seen to be the ultimate law

[4] New York: Charles Scribner's Sons, 1943, 1949, 1952, 1955 respectively.

of the universe. The Kingdom is the symbol referring to God's purpose for the whole of history, to the full "rule" of God, to an ultimate fulfillment and judgment of individual and social life. Within human history we can have only partial realizations of God's will; thus the Kingdom is "at the end of history," or "beyond history." Yet every partial achievement finds its meaning in the fullness of the Kingdom. In every decision men are confronted with the claim of God's rule. Thus the Christian lives both in response to God's rule now and in the hope of the final victory over evil.

Man and His Sin

For Niebuhr, a true view of the ethical situation of man must be grounded in the Christian understanding of human nature. Niebuhr's discussion of this theme in the first part of *The Nature and Destiny of Man* is perhaps his greatest contribution to recent thought. To many, his analysis there of man's responsibility and sin seems the most original and creative treatment of the matter in all modern theological literature.

Many people suppose that Niebuhr speaks of man simply as sinner. Nothing could be farther from the truth. On the contrary, Christianity for Niebuhr has a very "high estimate of human stature," for man is created in the image of God and is responsible to him. Christianity does, however, have a "low estimate of human virtue," for it recognizes that sin is universal—that is, when they are seen in the light of Jesus Christ, all men are judged to be sinners. It is important then to see how sin arises and the forms that it takes.

One must begin by seeing that man is a peculiar creature, both bound and free. He is part of nature and bound by natural processes; yet he rises above nature as a creature of reason, morality, and spirit. He is finite, limited, yet he is free, conscious of his limitations, and able to transcend mechanical or biological determination. And just this is the root of the difficulty. For man, knowing his limitation and his freedom, is inevitably concerned ("anxious") about himself.

Anxiety (in this special sense) comes with freedom; it is part of man's created existence. Anxiety is not sin. It makes possible *both* sin and faith. In his precarious situation, confronted with his limitation and his freedom, man may accept himself in his dependence upon God—this is faith. Or, man may deny his true creaturehood—this is sin, and Christian faith affirms that all men fall into sin. Sin is not just "wrong acts"; it is a distortion that comes at the center of the self. Sin is not necessary (man is not forced into sin), but it is universal.

Niebuhr suggests that sin may take two basic forms. Man may try to deny his freedom and responsibility, and retreat into simple animal nature. This form of sin is "sensuality." (It does not mean that the body is evil; the body is good, and the sin here is an act of freedom and spirit.) Or, man may seek to deny his limitations and to assert his independence. This is the sin of pride, which is the most basic and universal. It is, Niebuhr holds, the root of all sin. This is the opposite of faith, for it places ultimate trust in something less than God.

Niebuhr has explored the manifold forms of the sin of pride with uncommon insight and precision. His concern for realism in Christian action is intimately bound up with his awareness of the subtle forms that pride takes in its assertion of the self. There is the pride of power, of those who imagine themselves completely master of their own existence and destiny. There is the frantic will-to-power, which seeks final security in dominating others. There is the pride of intellect, or moral or spiritual pride, which thinks its own conceptions and ideals free from all taint of self-interest, and thereby assumes for itself divine authority.

For Niebuhr, the Christian doctrines of man and sin are not merely theoretical or abstract notions. They are indispensable tools for the understanding of every human situation. They are just as relevant for the social analyst and the political planner as for the theologian.

The same thing may be said about the doctrine of justification by faith, a theme that runs through all Niebuhr's concerns and brings them together. As we are all bound up in the manifold forms of sin, as our history finds fulfillment only in the kingdom of God, and as our efforts at justice and righteousness always involve compromise and only relative expression of the law of love—so we are justified not by our works but only as in faith we trust in the graciousness of God. Accepting his forgiveness in our confused and ambiguous situation, we have both hope and energy for our striving in the service of God.

FOR FURTHER READING

Reinhold Niebuhr, *An Interpretation of Christian Ethics* (New York: Harper & Brothers, 1935).

———, *The Children of Light and the Children of Darkness* (New York: Charles Scribner's Sons, 1944).

Charles W. Kegley and Robert W. Bretall, eds., *Reinhold Niebuhr: His Religious, Social, and Political Thought* (New York: The Macmillan Company, 1956).

D. B. Robertson, ed., *Love and Justice,* Selections from the Shorter Writings of Reinhold Niebuhr (Philadelphia: Westminster Press, 1957).

Reinhold Niebuhr, *Leaves from the Notebook of a Tamed Cynic* (Doubleday Anchor Book, 1957).

VI

Paul Tillich

BY ROBERT CLYDE JOHNSON

Christianity always has lived, from the moment of its inception, in conversation with the culture about it. When we look back across the centuries we can trace a zigzag movement in this conversation. There have been eras when the prime concern has been to converse with culture. Theology has utilized the insights and terminology of the cultural pattern to formulate Christian truth, and to communicate it to the generation which has been molded by the cultural complex. In other eras the movement has been in the opposite direction, away from the reigning cultural forms, in the effort to cut the Christian message free from entanglements and accretions which have threatened to hide or obliterate it. The former movement is called *synthesis* (a bringing together); the latter is called *diastasis* (a cutting apart).

The theology of Paul Tillich is the great monument of synthesis of the twentieth century. There are certain contemporary thinkers, such as Reinhold Niebuhr and the Swedish bishop Anders Nygren, whose

ROBERT CLYDE JOHNSON is professor of theology, Yale University Divinity School, New Haven, Conn.

major theological contribution has been of the nature of diastasis. They have labored long and hard to free the message of Christianity from what they feel to be "foreign" elements which it accumulated in the nineteenth and early twentieth centuries. Other theologians, such as Karl Barth and Emil Brunner, have played a dual role, both leading forth in the cutting-apart effort, and then laboring to lay the foundation for a new synthesis. Only Tillich among the major theologians may be fully described as a theologian of synthesis, one whose consuming desire has been to take seriously and utilize positively the cultural needs, patterns, and modes of expression in reformulating and attempting to communicate Christian truth.

Born in Germany in 1886, Paul Tillich came to America in 1933, having been dismissed from his teaching positions and forced to leave Germany because of his anti-Nazi political views. His distinguished teaching in this country took him to Harvard, where he lectured both to the undergraduates and to the students of the Harvard Divinity School, and finally back to the University of Chicago.

The Method of Correlation

Tillich's drive for synthesis determines the nature of his theological thought and the method which he follows. He calls his method "the method of correlation." In intention it is quite simple, although its basis and implications are deep and far-reaching. It swings upon two contentions: (1) that if theology is to be "saving theology" it must speak to *the situation* of man, his real, throbbing problems of life and death; and (2) that theology and philosophy are inseparable.

It is the first of these two convictions that casts the mood of Kierkegaard and contemporary existentialism over Tillich's thought, and has caused some to refer to his system as "existential theology." He insists that flesh-and-blood human existence, not abstract theory, is the soil which theology must plow. But for him, to speak of existential theology is like speaking of an albino white horse. He even contends that truth is not true—it matters not how well it may be formulated, or how closely it may conform to the Bible and traditional "orthodoxy"—unless it can be received by man, and can speak to his condition.

The structural basis of the method of correlation rests upon a serious trust in the trustworthiness of human reason. Ordinarily when we use the word "reason" we mean simply logical thinking; but by the word Tillich means more than just the process of human thought. He insists that the world is so created that it embodies certain "structures," and that these structures find their intended correspondence in the mind of man. It is when the structures of the mind meet the structures of objective, external reality that knowledge becomes possible. The term "reason," in Tillich's thought, refers to these structures of reality and of the mind, as well as to the thought process.

The technical word which Tillich uses for his assumption of these corresponding structures is *logos,* a Greek term which appears in the prologue of the Gospel of John (where it is translated as "Word"), and which has a long philosophical and theological history. This is the initial point where his entire theology joins hands with classical Greek philosophy.

The word *logos,* in its various forms, can be freely translated as "thought," "pattern of rationality," "reason," or "word." It is the term which is joined with the Greek word for God to make the word "theology." Theology is thinking or reasoning about

God. For Tillich, *logos* means reason, understood in the sense of the corresponding structures. It is his assumption of "the universality of the *logos*" which enables him to take human reason with total seriousness, and which lays the foundation for his theological method and system. Human reason, as such, cannot answer the ultimate questions which are raised by the mind of man; but reason can ask the questions, and the answers which are given, through revelation, come to man through this same reason. Thus he insists that question and answer not only may, but must, be correlated, wedded in an inviolable union, with each rooting in the universal *logos*.

The Human Situation

Tillich's theological system is in five parts. Each part consists of an ultimate question arising out of the human situation and developed philosophically, and then of the answer that comes through revelation. He recognizes that the question and the answer interact; but primarily the first half develops the existential "problem," and the last half the theological "solution."

What does Tillich say about the basic need of man to which Christianity must speak in our day? He insists that "it is not an exaggeration to say that today man experiences his present situation in terms of disruption, conflict, self-destruction, meaninglessness, and despair in all realms of life." He believes that the various forms of cultural expression offer infallible clues to the way in which man actually experiences his human situation, and thus he draws heavily upon depth psychology, existential philosophy, modern art and poetry, and political and historical fact in his analysis.

Man, he says, knows and feels himself to be confronted by "the threat of nonbeing," or of "not being." He discovers that he is a creature, wholly contingent, dependent upon and ruled by powers—both within and without—which he neither controls nor creates. This poses man's basic problem, which is his *finitude*. He knows the infinite; but he also knows in the same moment that he is not of the infinite. This knowledge comes to him in the form of a threat. Why should he be, and not not be? May he not, at any moment, cease to be? It is this underlying knowledge which forces man to recognize that anxiety is of the essence of his existence. This anxiety is neither temporary nor accidental. It is permanent and universal. This discovery points to his deepest need, a need for "the courage to be."

Why is it necessary to define man's very existence with the word "anxiety"? Man is created free and with unlimited possibilities open before him. "Possibility," Tillich says, "is temptation." As man acts, on the basis of the freedom which is the mark of his created nature, he turns away, and separates himself, from God. He does this (1) through self-elevation, as he makes himself his God; (2) through unbelief, as both with his mind and with his actions he denies his intended dependence upon God; and (3) by his unlimited striving, as he uses his potentialities without considering their source or the will of the God who gave them. Man's actual situation, therefore, must be described as one of primal *separation* (the word Tillich uses for the traditional word "sin"). Man has separated himself from the ground of his being, from his Creator, from the One who is intended to be his God.

The results of this separation are disastrous and all-pervasive. It creates a deep loneliness in human life that can never be overcome. It also results in an unavoidable blindness and a paralysis of the will.

In his separated condition man finds that he cannot escape involvement in both personal and collective "lies." He "labels" others, and refuses to look beneath the label. He tends to pervert and destroy everything, making it what from his estranged point of view he wishes it to be. When he is confronted with the necessity for decision, he tries to rid himself of the burden. He dissolves himself in a political movement, or in a social group, to hide his embarrassment in the face of recurring paralysis of the will. This turns him against himself, and against his fellowmen. His life becomes competitive rather than cooperative. This produces suffering, which he feels to be senseless suffering. The suspicion of meaninglessness creeps over him. Cynicism and despair, the "sickness unto death" of Kierkegaard, envelop him.

Every effort that man makes to overcome this situation is futile. It only serves to aggravate his condition and increase his separation, because the effort itself is based upon this condition of primal separation. Whenever and wherever man refuses to recognize this, and seeks to conquer his condition with moral striving, religious forms, or social and political programs, he merely inches more closely to the brink of annihilation. The undeniable and unshakable fact is that on the deepest level of his existence man is helpless and hopeless—except where he recognizes this helplessness and hopelessness, and thus seeks "New Being," or quests for "the Christ."

The Divine Answer

Human existence, trapped in this situation, cries out for "a reality of reconciliation and renewal, of creativity, meaning, and hope." This is precisely what is given to us, Tillich says, in "the picture of Jesus as the Christ" which we find in the New Testament. Here is the "new creation" for which we long. "If anyone is in Christ, he is a new creation," says Paul (II Corinthians 5:17). This "new creation" is described by Tillich as *New Being,* the pivotal concept of his entire theology. What we see in "the picture of Jesus as the Christ," he says, is manhood which is not cursed by the separation that disrupts and destroys our lives. He actualized his freedom, just as we do, and lived under all the conditions of our human existence; yet there is in him no trace of self-elevation, unbelief, or disregard of the giver of life and freedom. In his words, in his deeds, and in his suffering, there is an uninterrupted transparency to the ground of being, a continuous giving of himself to God. Here is "God-manhood," the fully human which has completely overcome all separation from "the divine ground."

This New Being, Tillich says, is "the principle of salvation." It is a power that liberates and transforms our separated and torn human existence, so that we participate in the "new creation." Under this power we are united with the ground of being, with God; our inner "split" is overcome, and we are made one again with one another. This is salvation, a healing which is a reunion beyond our separation.

How do we participate in this power of the New Being? Tillich's answer to the ancient question "What must I do to be saved?" [1] is "Nothing—literally nothing." It is, first and last, a matter of grace. It is only as we are "struck by grace" that the salvation, the healing of our separation and estrangement, becomes possible. This means that "faith" is not in any sense something that we can or may do, but is a *gift* that is given *in spite of* what we have done. We are

[1] Acts 16:30.

accepted by God—this is Christianity's message. It is here that we see how seriously Tillich has taken Luther, or how utterly Protestant he is. Nothing is quite so disconcerting to him as the American "activist" mentality, the compulsion to reduce all things to acts and activity. "Sin" and "grace" must each be understood as a "state" (" 'sin' should never be used in the plural!" he insists). Sin is the state of separation, and grace is the opposite of sin. "Grace is the reunion of life with life, the reconciliation of the self with itself." This is the New Being which is offered, a "new creation" for us. "It is as though a voice were saying: 'You are accepted. *You are accepted.* . . . Do not try to do anything now; perhaps later you will do much. Do not seek for anything. *Simply accept the fact that you are accepted!* " [2] He who hears this voice has been struck by the stroke of grace.

It is thus that the "walls of separation" are broken down. In the knowledge that we are accepted, we can accept ourselves. It then is possible for us to accept one another, without the aggressive bitterness and hostility that have plagued our lives. In so far as we are "in Christ," our estrangement from God, from ourselves, and from one another is overcome in the power of the New Being.

Questions

The theology of Tillich bristles with questions, both for the layman and for the theologian. The most nagging question for the layman is "Can I understand him?" His technical vocabulary is a language which is quite foreign to the rank and file of the church, although his books of sermons, *The Shaking*

[2] From *The Shaking of the Foundations,* by Paul Tillich. Copyright 1948, by Charles Scribner's Sons, New York.

of the Foundations and *The New Being,* are highly readable and very powerful.

Theologians have raised their most pointed questions about his "theological" use of philosophy, the nonpersonal tincture in his doctrine of God, and the fact that his analysis of man's dilemma seems to suggest that creatureliness is man's basic problem. Serious questions will also be raised about his doctrine of Christ and his interpretation of atonement. And, although his appointed task was philosophical theology, not biblical scholarship or biblical theology, the question remains whether or not he took seriously enough the essential Hebraic structure of biblical thought.

There is a wide and serious diversity of reaction to the thought of Tillich in the theological world. One theologian suggests that he was Protestantism's twentieth-century Aquinas; and another equally eminent authority said, "There is no more dangerous theological leader alive than Dr. Tillich." Whatever the verdict of history will be about him, it will include an unhesitant recognition that he was one of those rare and great minds which leave the whole of human civilization in their debt.

FOR FURTHER READING

Paul Tillich, *The Shaking of the Foundations* and *The New Being* (New York: Charles Scribner's Sons, 1948 and 1955, respectively). Sermons.

———, *The Courage to Be* (New Haven, Conn.: Yale University Press, 1952). A book worth trying.

Charles W. Kegley and Robert W. Bretall, eds., *The Theology of Paul Tillich* (New York: The Macmillan Company, 1952).

VII

Rudolph Bultmann

BY CARL MICHALSON

Rudolf Bultmann, a German New Testament scholar born in 1884, has made a major contribution to Christian thought with what he calls his "existential hermeneutics." All his theological novelties and accents originate here.

"Existential hermeneutics" is a complex label for what everyone does quite normally, and for what theologians must do somewhat studiously. Hermeneutics is the science of interpretation. Anyone who reads books does so with an implicit or explicit principle of interpretation. Whether his reading will be profitable does not depend entirely upon the book he is reading. It depends to a great extent upon how he interprets what he is reading. Hence, even though for Protestants the Bible is in principle the dominant norm of authority for the faith, it can actually have varying degrees of significance, depending upon one's method of reading it.

According to Bultmann, the Bible should be read

CARL MICHALSON until his death was professor of systematic theology at Drew Theological Seminary, Madison, N. J.

as any other piece of literature. If this is true, it could save Christians a great deal of trouble. They would not be involved in the endless hassle over the extent to which the Bible is a special kind of book. But how should "any other" book be read? One should enter into its point of view in such a way as to read it from the perspective of the book itself. *One should ask the questions of the book which the book itself is answering.* Therefore, one needs to ask the Bible what it is saying, and not impose upon it some presuppositions of one's own on the subject.

The remarkable thing about reading the Bible from the biblical point of view is that the Bible shows no interest in the facts of past history, or in theological data for their own sake. It rather exposes the life of the reader to the problem of his personal existence and directs him to a solution which rings with the ultimacy of God's own Word.

This suggests why Bultmann calls his principle of interpretation *"existential* hermeneutics." Hermeneutics is called existential simply because the Bible is found to appeal to the same dimensions of depth and self-understanding in men to which existential philosophy appeals. As the American poet Delmore Schwartz has put it, existentialism is the philosophy that believes no one can take your bath for you. Martin Heidegger, who was Bultmann's colleague at the University of Marburg for many years and a close collaborator, developed his existential philosophy around the theme that no one can die your death for you. Bultmann takes the position which he believes is held by existentialism because it was first held by Christianity: no one can hold your faith for you.

When a man reads the Bible from the point of view of the Bible and asks the fundamental questions about his own destiny, he hears the Word of God coming from the Bible as a call to complete obedience. His very life or death hangs upon his decision. The authentic response to the call to decision cannot be a body of data which describes what the Bible is saying. It must be a new and meaningful life. When this event takes place, revelation has occurred. Revelation is the event in which God's Word, communicated through the preaching of the church, constitutes one's life as meaningful. The Bible is the preaching in which the primitive church was born. It is the task of the church through the study of the Scriptures, through theology, and through preaching to let God's Word animate the church again.

Preachers have the easiest time doing this. Proclamation begets proclamation in their hands. Theologians and New Testament scholars have the hardest time. Biblical scholars tend to shy away from existential hermeneutics. They try to read the Bible from the standpoint of other books rather than from the standpoint of the Bible. They want to go behind the Bible to see what its sources are in climate, language, and religious history. In the very effort, they are in peril of separating themselves, their own meaningful lives, from the interpretative task—a procedure which the Bible itself does not endorse. Theologians, moreover, tend to substitute statements about the nature of revelation for the preaching in which the revelation comes to life. They talk about the Christ who is God's Word for us as if he were something in himself. Whereas, according to Bultmann, revelation is Jesus as the Word of God, the holy event of God for us, the event that makes our lives meaningful through this act of God.

The Structure Behind Bultmann's Method
of Interpretation

Bultmann takes his method of interpretation very seriously, and structures it with the help of certain philosophical ideas derived from existentialism.

The first idea coming out of existentialism has to do with *the intentional nature of consciousness.* Every act of consciousness is always a *consciousness of* something. Every subjective impression "intends" an objective correlate. However, in acts of understanding, it is the relation of the subject to the object that is investigated. It is then that the question of the existence of the object is bracketed, for it is a secondary consideration. Only the question of its meaning is raised, for the question of meaning is the juncture at which consciousness joins itself to the object contemplated. That relationship *is* the meaning. Meaning does not inhere either in the subject (how I feel) or in the object (what it is), but in the meeting between subject and object (what is meant).

The second rather sophisticated structure behind the Bultmann method is taken from existentialism's concept of time. "Time" for existentialists is divided into the customary categories of past, present, and future. But these do not mean for existentialism precisely what they do for common sense. If they did, the present would be a dimensionless mathematical point on a line separating past and future. As it is, for existentialism the present is the dimension in which a man really lives. It is the realm of one's meaningful life. It is what saves us from simply living in the past. Now the past is not, for existentialism, what it is for common sense. It is not simply that which has decidedly happened, once-for-all. It is a realm of inauthenticity, where no decisiveness, no freedom, no life resides. It is always the *"dead* past." What, then, is the possibility of a man's being saved from the dead past for life in a meaningful present? The future! The future is filled with hope. But because it is future, it is only possible. It is not necessary. Because it is only possible, one must decide about it. He cannot know the future in the same way that he knows what is already past.

Now for Bultmann, the holy event of saving knowledge which comes in God's revelation of his word is always in the future. It is what he calls an "eschatological event." By that he does not mean that the revelation never comes. Rather, it is the event which is always coming. In coming, it saves us from our inauthentic bondage to the dead past by delivering our lives into a meaningful present.

Bultmann's concept of history, which is crucial for an understanding of his position, is tied up with both these points: with his phenomenological theory of consciousness and with his existential view of time. History in modern times no longer means what it once meant for the historians. It does not mean "the facts of the past." As Goethe and Nietzsche established, there are no facts without interpretation. History is event interpreted—meaningful events. In the light of Bultmann's concept of consciousness and time, in what sense is Christianity historical?

Christianity is interpretation in which the holy event of God's revelation in Jesus Christ takes place. That revelation is an "eschatological event." That is, it is primarily future, a possibility to be decided in faith. It constitutes my present as meaningful when I interpret that event in an act of decision, an act of obedience, an act of faith.

Applying the Method

Here the real trouble begins, although it need not be trouble if one understands these methodological backgrounds. Was there an historical Jesus? This question compounds the problems. If by historical is meant a fact of the past, open to the scrutiny of the scientific historians, then Bultmann might say yes. He would hasten to add, however, that the Bible is interested not in the past history of Jesus but in his present Lordship. The key to that is in the fact that the Bible is not scientifically recorded past events. The literary form of the New Testament is evidence of that. It is proclamation of God's saving deed, the preacher's *interpretation* of the event of the past.

Bultmann was one of the pioneers in the development of this understanding of New Testament literature by the "form-history" school. When you read the New Testament you ought not to be interested in the factuality, the objectivity, the past existence of Jesus. If you are, you are not reading the Bible from the standpoint of the Bible. It is not that the objective facts are not there. It is rather that they are "put in parenthesis" in order to allow the meaningful relation to "happen." The Bible is not a record of events but an interpretation. When it is preached, that is, reinterpreted, it brings the saving event to life in the present. History in the New Testament sense is not an isolated objective event. It is not even an arena in which persons appropriate truths in eventful meetings. History *is* the meeting.

"Demythologizing"

That is not to say that there is not a great deal of past history in the New Testament. There is. It causes the biblical interpreter or the preacher his greatest problem. For alongside the preaching in the New

Testament (the technical name for this preaching is the *kerygma*) is another literary form, the myth (*mythos*). Preaching is a way of speaking about God's holy event so as to allow it to repeat itself in the present. Myth, however, in the sense in which it is used in the study of the history of religions, is a way of speaking of God's acts as if they are scientifically determinable events. But, says Bultmann, God's acts are always "eschatological events," events which are in history as possibilities for the constituting of our lives as meaningful. To talk about these holy acts in terms of their location in world space and in past time is to mythologize them.

Miracle stories, cosmological descriptions about how Jesus was born and how he will return, conjectures about the location of heaven and hell in terms of first-century astronomy, philosophies of history, psychophysical evidences of the resurrection, metaphysical speculation about the nature of God and man—all have myth in them. That is, they all step outside the preaching task of the Christian community where proclamation of saving knowledge is the sole burden and where the decisiveness of faith is the sole response. That is why Bultmann, a Lutheran, strongly influenced by the Pauline message of the New Testament, has been urging the preachers of Germany to "demythologize" the New Testament. (It is for this that he has become best known in recent years.) As Paul and Luther taught, justification is "by faith alone"; and to demythologize keeps one from commending justification on some other basis than faith. The mythologizing tendency of the New Testament tempts one to base his faith on historical facts of the past. A Christian, however, is called to base his faith upon the saving act of God which always comes to us as out of the future with no validation except the act of complete obedience in the decision of faith.

Evaluations

Many scholars believe that Bultmann is wrong to wish to demythologize the New Testament just at a time when poets and other artists have come to take up the New Testament myths as the religiously meaningful symbols for our time. Bultmann, however, does not mean by myth what the literary people do. The New Testament myths are not symbols which unite a man with his deepest meanings. Bultmann holds they are falsifications of meaning inasmuch as they tend to treat as scientific history what is really a revelational event. Though they have the intention of the Christian preaching, they are a device which obstructs and thwarts the radical obedience of faith. They drain off one's attention into the question of factualities and, in the process, defeat the artist's purpose, which is to answer the question about the meaning of life.

A great group of scholars believes that Bultmann represents a rebirth of nineteenth-century liberalism which called the New Testament a mythological document. Stripping away the mythological element, it found nothing of any great significance left. Bultmann, however, does not call for a stripping away of myth. Demythologizing does not mean throwing the myth away. It means *interpreting* the myth. In that sense, demythologizing is simply preaching again the gospel of the New Testament, releasing it from the world of the first century and getting it into the life of the present-day man.

Bultmann's demythologizing project (first published in 1941) was originally addressed to preachers. However, Bultmann believes that the New Testament scholars and theologians have one common task with the preacher: so to interpret the Bible that God's word may be heard today. Therefore, a great storm is rocking the theological world at this moment to determine whether a method which might have some justification for preachers can possibly be carried through by biblical and systematic theologians.

FOR FURTHER READING

Rudolf Bultmann, *Primitive Christianity* (Living Age Books, 1956).

———, *Jesus and the Word* (Charles Scribner's Sons, 1958).

———, *Kerygma and Myth* (Harper & Row, 1961).

VIII

Martin Buber

BY WALTER E. WIEST

Emil Brunner, in discussing the relation between "ordinary knowledge" and revelation, says that ordinary knowledge "is always knowledge of an object." Revelation involves "another kind of knowledge— that in which the other confronts me not as an object but as a subject, where he is no longer an 'It' but a 'Thou.' " [1]

Statements like this, using the term "Thou" or "I-Thou" to explain what Christians mean by revelation and faith, occur time after time in works by contemporary Protestant theologians and biblical scholars. What they mean can be understood best by reference to the thought of Martin Buber, the distinguished contemporary Jewish thinker, from whose writings this terminology is drawn. Buber has been so effective in reinterpreting for modern men what the Bible says about God, man, and the world that

WALTER E. WIEST is professor of philosophy of religion at Pittsburgh Theological Seminary, Pittsburgh, Pa.

[1] From *Revelation and Reason,* by Emil Brunner. Copyright 1946, by W. L. Jenkins, The Westminster Press, Philadelphia. Used by permission.

Christian writers have reached into his books and gratefully helped themselves.

In the background of Buber's thinking is a rather unusual form of Jewish faith, called Hasidism, which arose about 1750 in the isolated Jewish communities of Poland. Hasidism ("Hasid" means a holy or pious person) was an expression of a very warm, joyful, religious spirit. God was close and real, his presence felt, both in the close personal ties that bind men in genuine community and in a sense of intimate relation to nature.

At first, Hasidism, with its deep sense of the Divine presence in everything, led Buber into the study of mysticism. Biblical studies later turned his thought in new directions and helped him put in new perspective some other elements in Hasidic Judaism. In the Bible, Buber came to see, God confronts man in an intimate personal relationship in which there is a kind of conversation or "dialogue," a real give-and-take. From this comes a new understanding of faith and of religious truth or knowledge. What I believe or know is, in this sense, what *happens* to me when I meet with and respond to another in the fullness of his being *as a person*. This is precisely what the Bible means, says Buber, by revelation. It is not a set of propositions *about* God and man but a series of encounters *between* God and men. Faith, consequently, is not a matter of saying "yes" with the mind to certain "articles of faith" but a positive response of one's whole being to God who confronts him with a personal demand. The call of faith is not "Believe that certain things are so" but "Choose ye this day whom ye will serve," or "Come, follow me."

This sort of relation, to which Buber gives his famous label "I-Thou," calls for a much different way of looking at things than is customary with us.

Usually we consider things for their possible uses and feel we know them best by looking at them objectively and impersonally. This is roughly what scientific knowledge, in its efforts to classify things according to their general characteristics and interpret their behavior by laws of cause and effect, suggests to us. It involves a detached, uncommitted attitude to which Buber applies the term "I-It." We can take this attitude toward people as well as toward sticks and stones. For instance, we can classify man biologically (a thinking, vertebrate animal), pigeonhole him in the social structure (employee, draftee, social security No. 4001-226-839), or treat him as a means to an end (cheap labor, easy mark, eligible bachelor). Buber recognizes that some degree of impersonal structure is necessary to human culture. His point is that we readily forget the I-Thou underlying I-It relations.

In his much-quoted phrase, "All real living is meeting," Buber asserts the need of men to find fulfillment in I-Thou relations with others. The ideal type of I-Thou relationship might be the best moments of a good marriage, in which each partner gives himself to the other unselfishly and yet finds fuller life in the giving. What happens, happens *between* them, in their relation. No one can sustain such a relation permanently, but it can be constantly renewed. And wherever a true I-Thou encounter occurs, there God is present also, whether recognized consciously or not. In every meeting with a "Thou," we meet "the eternal Thou."

The Dialogue of Faith

There are three respects in which Buber contributes especially to Protestant faith. One is his interpretation of the "prophetic" character of biblical faith. It is all too easy for "I-It" thinking to invade religion itself. It can happen when we indulge in traditional theological language about God (he is infinite, eternal, immutable, omniscient, et cetera). It happens when we reduce faith to ritual and moral law, thinking that when we have attended services and paid our respects to decency we have fulfilled our obligations and can turn to other concerns. It happens when we identify faith with acceptance of the letters on the pages of Scripture; Buber has helped us to understand how to take the Bible seriously without forgetting that it is "the letter that killeth, the Spirit that maketh alive."

By contrast, prophetic faith catches up the individual in a vivid, lively "dialogue." There are no formulas to follow, but a constant calling for new decision. God even extends to men the freedom to argue with Him. In his book *A Prophetic Faith,* Buber describes Jeremiah standing before God "lamenting, complaining to God himself, disputing with Him about justice. . . . Man can speak, he is permitted to speak; if only he truly speaks to God, then there is nothing he may not say." [2] In relation to God, it is better to be honestly hostile than dishonestly respectful or indifferent: "If there were a devil, it would not be one who decided against God, but one who, in eternity, came to no decision." [3]

His Concept of Community

Buber's second great contribution is in the understanding of human relations. The chief respect in

[2] From *A Prophetic Faith,* by Martin Buber. Copyright 1949, by The Macmillan Company, New York. Used by permission.

[3] From *I and Thou,* by Martin Buber. Copyright 1937, by Charles Scribner's Sons, New York. Used by permission.

which Buber differs from other "existentialist" thinkers from Kierkegaard to Sartre is that he never runs the risk of leaving the individual isolated. In the shaping of his own destiny, in relation to God, the self is at the same time related to others. Hasidism had a warm feeling for what happens "between man and man" in intimate religious community. Prophetic faith adds a sense of God's claim upon the whole life of a people. Buber says, for instance, that Old Testament injunctions against the oppression of widows, orphans, or "sojourners" are addressed to the whole community of the "people of God." They cannot be a "people" when "the social distance loosens the connections of the members of the people and decomposes their direct contact with one another." God "does not want to rule a crowd, but a community." [4]

Buber sees modern man caught in a dilemma, swinging from a radical individualism (every man for himself) to a radical collectivism (every man for the state or party). Neither has proved an answer to the terrible depersonalizing tendencies of modern society, with its bureaucracies, its technological gadgets, its emphasis on life in the mass. Against these, Buber offers a concept of community based on I-Thou relations. Recognizing another as "Thou" means feeling a responsibility for him. As it is expressed in *Between Man and Man,* "A newly-created concrete reality has been laid in our arms; we answer for it . . . a child has clutched your hand, you answer for its touch; a host of men moves about you, you answer for their need." Thus is community created. Community "is the being no longer side by side but

[4] From *A Prophetic Faith,* by Martin Buber. Copyright 1949, by The Macmillan Company, New York. Used by permission.

with another . . . a flowing from I to *Thou.* Community is where community happens." [5]

Buber has tried to apply his thinking in some interesting experiments with community life in the new Israel. Protestants might well remember that a distinctive thing about New Testament Christianity was its expression in a new community love. Men need community; they can be lost in a crowd. Yet Protestant churches are faced with their own problems of bureaucracy, highly geared programs, congregational life which often seems anything but warm, dedicated, and alive. Where should we look for the kind of Christian community that is created when men respond in faith to God's coming in his Word?

In the World of Nature

The third contribution of Buber can be only suggested here. There are difficult passages in which Buber says that, just as one can have I-It relations with persons, he can also have I-Thou relations with impersonal things. This is the continuing "mystical" strain in his thinking which he never wholly lost from Hasidism. What Buber seems to mean is that anything—a tree, a dog—may manifest itself to us as a part of God's creation in which God himself is actively present. This causes us to take things seriously for what they are in themselves, not only for what *use* they may be to us.

Protestant thought has been relatively weak in an understanding of nature and of science. It has tended often to abandon the field to naturalistic or pantheistic philosophies. Buber's I-Thou may open the way to a new interpretation of nature and a new way of

[5] From *Between Man and Man,* by Martin Buber. Copyright 1955, by Beacon Press, Boston, Mass. Used by permission.

relating a Christian view of creation to scientific knowledge. What he suggests is that although scientific knowledge of a tree is good and necessary, after such analysis we still have to put the pieces back together, so to speak, and see the tree again as an entity in its own right. But this occurs in a relation to things that is more like the communion we have with a "Thou" than it is like detached scientific objectivity. The world then appears as a "spiritually responsive universe," in the words of another writer.

This is not to say that trees are persons, or that one will necessarily find God if he is moved by beautiful sunsets. Buber is saying rather that the God whom we know primarily and fundamentally in personal encounter can also be met as "the eternal Thou" throughout all his creation. This may help Protestants to recover something of the sense of the mystery of God's presence in all things which has often been obscured in the emphasis upon individual faith and practical morality.

Buber has always remained faithful to Judaism. Christians cannot claim him in this sense, but it is remarkable how much he can offer us from the perspective of his own Jewish faith. One of the things gained in biblical studies in recent years is a renewed appreciation of the distinctively Hebrew foundations of Christianity. We should be able to appreciate more than ever the truth of the statement that spiritually we in the West are all Semites. With something of Buber's own profound respect for the Christianity he cannot accept, Christians can respond to him in appreciation and gratitude.

FOR FURTHER READING

Will Herberg, ed., *The Writings of Martin Buber* (Meridian Books, 1956). Contains parts of *I and Thou*, Buber's basic work.

Martin Buber, *Between Man and Man* (Boston: Beacon Press, 1956).

IX

Dietrich Bonhoeffer

BY THEODORE A. GILL

Dietrich Bonhoeffer was born February 3, 1906. His continuing story, however, can start just as well now as then. For, the farther we get from his death on the Nazi gallows, April 9, 1945, the clearer it becomes that Bonhoeffer's own singular activity will be given new extensions and expansions in all the years ahead. A prisoner who was with the young German pastor when he was summoned to his execution remembers Bonhoeffer murmuring "This is the end—for me the beginning . . ." The phrase is not characteristic; it is a little too self-conscious, self-dramatizing, and even traditionally "religious" sounding for the powerful, independent, and personally reticent Bonhoeffer. But, insofar as his career in this world goes, the phrase has turned out to have had an uncanny accuracy.

The Bonhoeffer story and significance are extended, for instance, wherever and whenever our latter-day radicals appeal to his writing for the solid

THEODORE A. GILL is Executive Director of the Society for the Arts, Religion, and Contemporary Culture. Former president of San Francisco Theological Seminary and managing editor of *Christian Century*.

support and flinty edge he gives there to the most extreme and violent measures necessary to blast away impacted evil in emergency situations. Haranguers and plotters, black and white, regularly appeal to Bonhoeffer's ethics for Christian justification of their radically disruptive strategies. And in the writing of this extraordinary Lutheran, they find what their desperation needs.

Right alongside the violent, sharing their ends but condemning their means, are campus pacifists, young men and women as humiliated and infuriated as are their more incendiary contemporaries by the evil rampaging in our midst, but determined that their own resistance must be nonviolent, must be stubbornly, self-sacrificially noncooperative with the evil. And these meek, too, can look to Dietrich Bonhoeffer's example and books for confirmation of their grimly insistent gentleness.

Meanwhile, good Christian folk (almost as apt to be offended by conscientious objectors as by bomb throwers, and unaware of Bonhoeffer's possible identification with both groups!) gratefully assemble in "spiritual life" groups and Lenten meditations to concentrate on two of his books: *The Cost of Discipleship* and *Life Together*. These, almost from time of publication, have been recognized as worthy additions to the glowing treasury of devotional classics. In them are the familiar discomforts and elevations of spiritual discipline featured in all such classics. The rigors and vigors of Christian demand are chastening, of course; that is part of what this kind of literature is about. But the same rigors and vigors are exalting, too (of us, so much can be expected); that is part of what this kind of literature is about, as well. And Bonhoeffer's middle books fit the genre splendidly.

Not all who glory in those classics, though, will feel easy about what happens to *Life Together* when it is read in youthful communes, where it can and does have "life-style" suggestions little appreciated in most parish spiritual life groups. Even less will some parishioners appreciate the development given Bonhoeffer's subsequent writing. Exactly where spiritual discipline still has a traditional definition, "situational ethics" is a dirty word. Yet this same Dietrich Bonhoeffer, who understood so specifically, so forcefully, so biblically the cost of discipleship, is inarguably also a father of situation ethics, of the kind of Christian morality which is not satisfied to memorize biblical injunctions and try to retrace them, but which also remembers the God met in Jesus Christ, assesses the possibilities in the situation demanding decision now, and improvises a moral activity which is as appropriate as possible at this moment to the eternal will of God.

Even where *Honest to God*—John Robinson's artful blend of Bonhoeffer, Bultmann, and Tillich—was taken in stride, the "Death of God" wasn't. Yet that extreme theology, too, looked back to certain of the most enigmatic passages in the letters Bonhoeffer wrote from prison near the end of his life.

All of this, and more (add the youthful diaries and lecture notes, and you can find encouragement for anti-Versailles German nationalism—but never Naziism—and antipacifism) from one man in one short life: the first influential look, *Cost of Discipleship,* was published in 1937, and the last line we have from Bonhoeffer's hand is in a letter to his parents in the first days of 1945.

A Man of His Times

Those who would understand Bonhoeffer must know his life and times. Only an understanding of the glue-tight correlation between world politics, personal developments, and theological reflections can put integrity into the fascinating sprawl of Bonhoeffer's ideas. It is not fair to him to try to give his work cohesion by detecting in it the consistent dominance of one motive or another (his Christology, or his ecclesiology, for example): that way obscures the radical novelty of his latest ideas, without which novelty he has no claim at all to our special attention. Neither is it fair to make him consistent by concentrating on his most radical last ideas and dismissing everything that went before as irrelevant: that way blurs the half-understood mystery of his final utterances which is a large part of their fascination, and misses completely the depths exposed and the pathos always involved in the wrenching of dearly held conviction.

In Bonhoeffer we have dramatic illustration of an understanding of the relation between thought and action that has since his death become standard for new generations of his admirers. Where once the ideal was carefully reasoned doctrine first, with appropriate action hopefully ensuing, Bonhoeffer is typical of more recent generations in acting first in ways appropriate to his nurture and his opportunity, and then making his theology an attempt to understand the action and its implications. The consistency in the breathtaking variety of his views is the consistency of one brilliant, honest man trying to make sense of and to deal responsibly with the life he loved (that gift of God) in the turbulences and inexplicabilities of a history both happier and more hideous than that given to most men.

The happiness came first (and it lasted to the end). Life was comfortable and pleasant in the family homes. For winter there was the great house in an elegant quarter of Berlin; for summer a rustic retreat in the meadows, woods and mountains. Dr. Karl Bonhoeffer, the father, was professor of psychiatry (vigorously anti-Freudian) at the University of Berlin; Mrs. (Paula von Hase) Bonhoeffer, whose relatives were counts and countesses, managed smoothly her large family and numerous servants. The eight Bonhoeffer children were a remarkably close company, enlarged gradually by the close friends who finally became the sisters' and brothers' husbands and wives. Dietrich, his twin sister, Sabine, and the baby of the family, Suzanne, were "the little ones" in the clan, but all were included in the games, the music, the parties, the travel, the joyous affections—as well as the polite order and intellectual discipline—of a great family.

The household was not notably religious. The conventional Bible-story Christian nurture was supplied in the children's early years, the two governesses were pious young women, a simple blessing was always asked at table—and that was it. Dr. Bonhoeffer and the older children were all of scientific or legal bent; an unaggressive agnosticism prevailed among them.

Dietrich's decision, when he was about fifteen, to major in theology was something new in the family, but not without precedent; earlier generations had included distinguished theological scholars. Besides, studying theology for a youth of Dietrich's obvious brilliance could only mean that he would himself teach theology at the university when his own studies were completed. To a university family, preparation for a professorial chair in any ancient faculty was understandable. So Dietrich's decision was taken in stride. Only lawyer brother Klaus, with no wish to discredit theology, worried about the waste involved in bright Dietrich signing up with as "peripheral" an outfit as the church is in the twentieth century.

Theological studies began for Dietrich at the University of Tübingen. After a year there, and a marvelous summer with Klaus in Rome and Northern Africa, Dietrich moved back to the family home in Berlin, and to the world-famous theological faculty at the capital's university. There he learned liberal theology from its master teachers—above all, Adolf von Harnack. Instruction was rigorous, exacting and wide-ranging: languages, history, texts. Interpretation was optimistic, evolutionary, progressive. An increasingly educated humanity, guided and encouraged by God and the exemplary Jesus, was seen to be refining and engineering its way onward and upward to the kingdom of God which men would finally build on earth. The talk was of ideals and values; the clues to the evolutionary will of God were abundant in nature, history, and conscience.

Then, sometime during his years at the University of Berlin, Bonhoeffer began to read Karl Barth. The earlier chapter on Barth in this book (Chapter IV) will already have made it clear why there was no rejoicing in the Berlin theological faculty when the most promising student around found swift affinity with the Swiss theologian's teaching. To Barth, Harnack and his colleagues "reduced Christianity to the noblest of man's sentiments." Against them, Barth called for a wondering advance into "the strange new world of the Bible," where God is no aspect of the universe, no ideal or value felt or deduced, but the living, judging, loving, free Person met in Jesus Christ; where men are not simply not yet as good as they are going to be, but are sinners going the wrong way; where God's will is not discernible in natural law or historical development or human conscience, but only in his Word, Jesus Christ; where the Kingdom of God is not something we build here, but something God delivers where and when and as he chooses.

It was all bracing, exciting, radical doctrine. In that dazzling episode in cultural history which was the Weimar Republic of the 1920's, with novelty crackling in architecture, painting, sculpture, drama, film, letters, the Barthian development of a brilliantly sophisticated primitivism as devastatingly self-confident and pugnacious as the Bauhaus or Brecht ever were, was religion's only interesting new entry. Dietrich Bonhoeffer went for it, hook, line, but not sinker. Bonhoeffer remained for long Barth's admiring, devoted, believing, *independent* disciple. To appreciate any of Bonhoeffer's books, Barth must be read first. To the end, though increasingly critical, Bonhoeffer knows God only in Christ, takes his moral lead from no principle but only from the Word especially focused on the particular issue.

Bonhoeffer finished his degree work in the expected blaze of glory. The highly technical thesis *Sanctorum Communio* confirmed his scholarship and his imagination, though by itself it would never have established his reputation. Before being ordained and beginning his own teaching, Bonhoeffer had to work for a year as an assistant in a parish. This he arranged to do in Barcelona. Typically, the year in Spain was full of travel (often with Klaus), music, tennis and swimming, as well as youth leading, teaching, and occasional preaching. The notes left from his lecturing show him at this stage an energetically patriotic German, increasingly indignant over the humiliating and oppressive terms of the Versailles treaty. As a good Barthian, militantly against ethical "principle," he opposes Tolstoyan pacifism. As a Lutheran as well as a Barthian, he summons the church to a purification of its own teaching and an avoidance of competition with the world in the world's business.

Even yet, it was not time to take up his university teaching post. From Union Theological Seminary in New York City came a fellowship for a year's graduate study. So, with the permission of church and school, Bonhoeffer was off for America, there to spend the 1930–31 academic year.

He was fascinated by the United States, critical of its theological education and churchmanship, and appalled by the abscess of its race relations. Driving through East, Midwest, and South, visiting both Cuba and Mexico, the learned young tourist gloried in the spaces and varieties in a continent new to him. He was less impressed by the shallowness of American theology and what seemed to him the naïve liberalism of his fellow students. Among them, he vigorously expounded and defended a pure-quill Barthianism. He was nonplused by the kind of storefront activism, neighborhood social work, and political involvement which has apparently always been native to Union students. The zeal was admirable, but what this direct social engagement had to do with the church was not clear to a 1930-model German Lutheran Barthian.

What was clear to him at that time was the criminal responsibility of white Protestants for what they had allowed to happen to black Americans. He was not sure, even then, that American Protestantism could survive its guilt history. His own happiest hours in the American church were spent with a beloved black fellow student in Harlem parishes. His most prized souvenir of the American adventure was the stack of recorded Negro spirituals that went back to Germany with him.

He also took back with him troubled reflections on pacifism. Personally committed to nonviolence, but theologically averse to elevating *any* principle to Gospel level, he could not agree simply with his new pacifist friends any more than he could with his new parish activist friends. But neither would he forget them. And long second thoughts were on their way.

Resistance Begins

The Germany to which Dietrich Bonhoeffer returned in 1931 was already racing toward the fatal embrace with fascism which would come in January, 1933. While the nation sickened around him, Bonhoeffer began his university teaching, and embarked on the ecumenical conference-going which was to involve him all over Europe for the next decade, representing youth in the planning for what would finally be the World Council of Churches. In these preliminary ecumenical jockeyings, Bonhoeffer was predictably purist in his theological demands. He was as insistent as Barth himself that the ecumenical church be more concerned to cure itself of its prenatal sickness (nineteenth-century liberalism) than to find ideal structures. But this theological concern was not as abstract as it may now sound. It was practical, political in the extreme. For it was liberalism's readiness to see and hear God in culture, history, and special personages that was disarming the German church before the Nazi claims. So Bonhoeffer, pushing Barthian Christocentrism, was not just making academic points. In insisting on Jesus Christ as the *only* source of our knowledge of God, as our *only* savior, Bonhoeffer was also denying the claim of any other national movement or charismatic politician to be a special revelation of God or a new agent of redemption. In the 1930's, when either Barth or Bonhoeffer spoke of Jesus Christ they were also saying a hard, negative thing about Adolf Hitler and the Nazi claims.

As a matter of fact, Bonhoeffer was cut off the air one day after Hitler came to power. The radio lecture was against the "leadership" principle so precious to the Nazis, and from the moment of his abrupt censoring Bonhoeffer was a marked man. His subsequent activity only fattened his file at Gestapo headquarters. While the National Socialist government tried to cajole or to coerce the German church into unquestioning allegiance to and cooperation with the new regime, Bonhoeffer went with Karl Barth, Martin Niemöller, and their friends in resistance to the state's plans to dominate and silence the church. Now the Barthian theology which had looked for a while so quietistic (with its concentration on the purifying of the church's own teaching) was suddenly embroiled in political controversy, not because the churchmen had changed course, gone political, but because national politics had pushed its own heretical claims into the theological sanctuary. Bonhoeffer's record was only further blackened by his increasingly pacifistic counsel at ecumenical gatherings. What might have sounded like a sweet Christian ideal outside Germany was recognized by the nation's scheming leaders for what it was meant to be by Bonhoeffer: an appeal for immediate resistance to the militaristic and international violence that all the

Bonhoeffers always knew were in the Nazi plans for their world.

The German church split, one part standing with the government, and a breakaway part (the Confessing Church) organizing to defend its structural and theological freedom. Bonhoeffer was in the midst of the furor. Then, in 1933 he left Germany again, this time for a two-year stay as the pastor of two German congregations in London. Barth was furious with what he regarded as his young affiliate's defection. Bonhoeffer worried about his own decision, promised not to stay long, used his time to get the Confessing Church a hearing abroad that it otherwise might not have had, and developed those ecumenical friendships which were to be all-important in later years. And, what may have weighed most of all with Bonhoeffer, he helped establish an escape route for his dearest friend at the time, Franz Hildebrandt, Jewish Lutheran pastor in increasingly hostile Berlin. It will not do to understand Bonhoeffer simply as theological prodigy or political hero. With him the most intimate motivations are transparently the most powerful. His chosen theology could not completely account for the fact, but it was family, friends, affections that moved him most.

At Finkenwalde

By 1935 the Confessing Church had to have Bonhoeffer back. Seminaries were to be established for this church-on-its-own, and the young university teacher (he resumed lecturing at the University of Berlin now) was recalled to be dean of the unobtrusively established theological school at Finkenwalde, northeast of Berlin. It was the two years at Finkenwalde that produced the two books which so quickly became devotional classics (especially in America),

The Cost of Discipleship and *Life Together.* It is exactly the sound of traditional spiritual discipline that makes these books popular with many, though that embarrasses Bonhoeffer scholars most acutely.

The scholars are embarrassed because, in tracing Bonhoeffer's theological development before Finkenwalde, it seems clear that he was already groping for theological expansions that would explain better to him than Barth did the high valuation that he naturally, invariably, ineradicably put on the world and its cultural activities. Then suddenly, at Finkenwalde, the older, more traditional sound was back. The high morality sounded like counsels of perfection; the gaze was often inward; everything seemed more for the church than the world. Worried commentators now refer to this whole Finkenwalde period, with its representative writing, as a detour. Later, Bonhoeffer would resume his movement into the world. Finkenwalde, they suggest, is an inexplicable siding. He would get back on the main line of his true development later.

But once again, the clue to interpretation is in the situation surrounding the writing. Bonhoeffer was offended, sickened, appalled by what was happening to Germany, and what he was always sure this abruptly ignoble state would do to the world. He was terrified by the threat to beloved relatives and friends. There never was any question about Bonhoeffer's resistance to the blight that was now settling on the splendid old culture. Dietrich Bonhoeffer, as a Barthian pastor, however, felt that his resistance had to be carried out within the church. Only when the insane state invaded the church would the Barthian churchman spring to the (strictly ecclesiastical) barricades. But Bonhoeffer knew that even if Hitler himself might have waited to take on the

church, his henchmen would begin at once their
effort to mold the church into National Socialism's
cultural homogenization. To withstand that, resisting
clergymen of the Confessing Church would have to
be steeled in their purpose. So Finkenwalde was the
boot camp for young ministers, drilled, hardened,
seasoned there by Bonhoeffer for the church fight
already in process. No wonder his teaching was more
interior, "spiritual," almost perfectionist, nearly
pacifist at Finkenwalde; he knew what the cost of
discipleship was going to be.

The government was very aware of Bonhoeffer.
Gradually his freedoms were limited; he couldn't pub-
lish, finally, or preach, or live in Berlin (he got permission to visit, though). He lost his lectureship at
the University of Berlin. Then Finkenwalde was
closed by the Gestapo. For a while Bonhoeffer continued his clandestine teaching even farther out in
the back country. He and his students arranged
appointments as assistant ministers in a couple of
remote parishes, and Bonhoeffer chugged around on
his motorcycle to hold classes in woods and fields,
out of sight.

Government pressure continued to build, however.
The issue of Bonhoeffer's registration for the military
draft couldn't be dodged much longer. The belea-
guered Confessing Church didn't need one more
contention with the state, especially about the conscientious objection of its already suspect young
teacher. So when a chance came for Bonhoeffer to
go again to New York, he was encouraged to leave.
Within days after his arrival in America, though, he
knew he had made a mistake. Agonized by the
danger he knew his family and friends to be in, un-
comfortable in his own safety, feeling cut off when
letters were delayed, he decided to return to Ger-

many. (The decision was made late one hot July
night while Bonhoeffer paced around Times Square.)

But he did not return to his original resistance in
Germany. Shortly, the classes in the woods were
suspended by the Gestapo. When the war began,
with the invasion of Poland, young resistance ministers were sent at once to die in the front lines; Barth
had had to leave Germany and was now in Switzerland; Martin Niemöller and other Confessing Church
leaders were in concentration camps; and the Confessing Churchmen left were too busy with pastoral
work in their alternately exalted and stricken parishes
to worry much about resistance. Besides, now that
war was declared, resistance to the government was
treason.

So Bonhoeffer had to relocate his resistance. He
did not have far to look. If the church's resistance
crumpled, then he would go into direct political resistance. He would join the plotters against Hitler—
one of the chief of whom was his brother-in-law,
Hans von Dohnanyi.

Political Action

Hans' conspiratorial cell was located within the
military intelligence service! Dietrich, in joining that
service (the Abwehr), was ostensibly in the spying
apparatus for the German military establishment,
though he was actually working against the head of
state—a kind of double agent. It was a bizarre ar-
rangement. The Gestapo, still suspicious of Bonhoeffer but unaware as yet of the conspiratorial nest
in the Abwehr, made life more and more difficult for
the young preacher. Yet at the same time the high-
placed conspirators were arranging permits and visas,
so the Dietrich Bonhoeffer who was hounded in
Germany moved more freely than almost any other

German citizen then, back and forth across borders
to Switzerland and Sweden carrying news of the conspiracy to the Allies, and trying to get Allied leaders
to give him encouraging, cooperative words for the
conspirators. He was a natural for this assignment
because he was known and trusted by the international churchmen who had become friends during
his New York and London years, and in all the years
of his ecumenical conference-going.

The Ethics

While danger and excitement built, some theological writing got done, too. There was large rethinking
to be done. Bonhoeffer had exchanged the indirect
resistance within the church for very direct political
plotting, pacifistic leanings for the possibility of
violence (even assassination), careful purity for "the
great masquerade of evil." Separate chapters of what
later was gathered and published as *Ethics* show
Bonhoeffer feeling his way toward brand-new theological orientation and formulations.

In the guise of technical theologizing, the *Ethics*
is a powerfully anti-Nazi document (though the
author knew it could never be published in Nazi
times). All the main illustrations of ethical issues
come from Nazi policy: war, militarism, genocide,
euthanasia, suicide, etc. The specific occasion must
be remembered whenever the *Ethics* is read and
interpreted. It is a part of Bonhoeffer's resistance.
But it is also this importance of the specific occasion
which gives the book wider, longer importance. For
it was while Bonhoeffer was trying to explain his own
participation in the lying and double-dealing of
traitors that he developed the beginnings of what has
since become known as situational or contextual
ethics: the right and the good and the true seen not as

immutable objectivities, but as qualities of any action which is as appropriate to the loving will of God as the particular possibilities in the immediate situation permit.

With terrible abruptness, the dramatics of conspiracy were over for Dietrich and Hans. Before any plots had jelled, before Dietrich's engagement to the beautiful young Ruth von Wedemyer could be announced (there had been only a few months of courtship), before the *Ethics* were anywhere near finished, Dietrich and Hans were arrested, never to return to their homes. For the first year, imprisonment was a nerve-racking time, spent trying to protect secrets while forcing a trial that might free the brothers-in-law. After July 20, 1944, however, simple survival was more than many could connive for. The failure of the attempt on Hitler's life that day uncovered deep hidden connections between conspirators. In a fury, Hitler put Bonhoeffer and von Dohnanyi on his list of criminals who must "under no circumstances be allowed to live." Execution was delayed, however, until all possible information had been extorted from them.

The Prison Letters

Bonhoeffer's theological adventures picked up as his conspiratorial ones slowed and stopped. In letters written to his best friend, Eberhard Bethge (whose big biography of Bonhoeffer is indispensable), the grounded theologian still so much on the move pushed into areas he hoped he would have time to reconnoiter more carefully after the war.

He wondered, for instance, what it should mean to think and preach and live as a Christian in "a world come of age." The phrase never meant to him a world without problems, needing no advice. Since when did coming of age mean that for anyone? He did mean, though, that the world's disciplines are competent now, are rightly on their own, in most areas where the church used to have to give the answers. So where does the church come in now? And with what?

Surely not with more cant about "the God of the gaps," the God we roll together to plug into any hole in our present knowledge—a God who is diminished every time we learn something more, do something great.

Neither will we talk in this new world about a God way out on the dismal edges of existence, a God good for sin and death only, and invoked in crisis if at all. The only God worth talking about now is one who is inescapably met everywhere, in every problem and delight and activity, met and served here and now, a presence and a charge in the thick of immediacy.

But he is not there as the grand lord of the manor. The oriental potentate must drop out of our theological models. His majesty is not in the flash of omnipotence, but is in the sovereignty of his suffering. His weakness, his sacrifice, is his greatness.

There are intriguing lines in the *Letters from Prison* about a "religionless Christianity," a "nonreligious interpretation of the Gospel." Radical commentators have run with those phrases, and to deny them that right is only to make Bonhoeffer safer, more ordinary. But there is so much else in the *Letters* that we do not have to buy the radical interpretation, either. Even his own most mysterious statements are surrounded as by halos with the scriptural, poetic, devotional utterances of the most traditional piety.

So Dietrich Bonhoeffer remains the glowing person, the enigmatic thinker, both still somehow vibrating ideas and events around us. He himself didn't make it. Days before the end of the war, just before Hitler's death and President Roosevelt's, with Germany in ruins, the dictator already sunk in his bunker and the sound of American guns clear in the prison's air, Dietrich Bonhoeffer, his brother Klaus, his brothers-in-law Hans von Dohnanyi and Rüdiger Schleicher, all were destroyed by their maniac keepers.

Bonhoeffer's death, of course, helps account for the attention given to his ideas. But their continued influence has just as obviously come from their own appositeness. He did not have time to find the answers to his own questions. But he movingly certified himself as appropriate comrade to all of us who find our questions in his, and go on looking.

FOR FURTHER READING

There are a number of books about Dietrich Bonhoeffer. The definitive biography is likely to be Eberhard Bethge's large volume *Dietrich Bonhoeffer,* published in 1970 by Harper & Row. In addition, the reader will profit from Mary Bosanquet, *The Life and Death of Dietrich Bonhoeffer* (Harper & Row, 1968).

The basic writings of Bonhoeffer, named and discussed in this article, are all available. *Letters and Papers from Prison* is a paperback. It was at one time called *Prisoner for God,* but later the publisher reverted to the earlier title.

X

Martin Heidegger

BY JOHN MACQUARRIE

Martin Heidegger is counted among the most creative philosophers of the twentieth century. Born in 1889 at Messkirch in the Black Forest region of Germany, he studied philosophy at the University of Freiburg and was profoundly influenced by Edmund Husserl, the founder of phenomenology. After a time as professor at the University of Marburg, Heidegger returned to Freiburg in 1929 to succeed Husserl, and most of his life has been spent in Freiburg or at his neighboring mountain retreat.

Early in his career, Heidegger became fascinated with a question which continued to dominate his thinking—*the question of the meaning of being*. This was the question which stimulated the philosophers of an earlier time, but more recently it has been neglected or even dismissed as a pseudo-question. Yet we can hardly utter two sentences without making use of the verb "to be" in one or other of its parts. What does it mean "to be"? It is hardly an answer to say that the meaning is self-evident or that

JOHN MACQUARRIE is Lady Margaret Professor of Divinity, University of Oxford, England.

this verb is merely a grammatical or logical device or that being is indefinable. From a philosophical point of view, such answers can be regarded only as evasive. The business of philosophy is to probe more deeply into what common sense accepts as self-evident, conventional or indefinable.

Heidegger's exploration into the question of being has fallen into two distinct phases. It has indeed become customary to talk of the early Heidegger and the later Heidegger and of the "turn" which separates the two phases of his philosophical work. However, the opposition between the two should not be exaggerated, as the same fundamental question dominates both phases. In the first phase, Heidegger believed that the question of being is best approached by an investigation into the being of man, as the existent who raises the question. Would not a study of the existence in which we share and which we know at first hand lead to an understanding of being in the widest sense? This approach guided Heidegger in the writing of his greatest work, *Being and Time* (1927). Yet even at that stage, Heidegger was aware that the being of man cannot be properly grasped apart from an understanding of being in general, so that one is already involved in a reciprocal act of interpretation, sometimes called the "hermeneutic circle." Thus he eventually acknowledged that the path which he had mapped out for himself in *Being and Time* could not be pursued to the end, though he also insisted that it is a path which must be trodden in any inquiry into being. In the later phase of his work, he has confronted the problem of being more directly. Instead of seeking to construct a concept of being through the exploration of his own being, man must rather listen to the voice of being as it addresses him. In Heidegger, language becomes increasingly important as the vehicle for the self-revelation of being.

The Starting Point Is Man

Only if we confined our attention to the first phase of Heidegger's philosophy could we call him an existentialist. But even so, the term would be inadequate, for he was never concerned with analyzing the being of man for its own sake, but only as laying the groundwork for the broader inquiry into the meaning of being in general. This was made very clear by Heidegger in his differentiation of his own position from Sartre's. Whereas the latter taught that the human existent is the creator of meaning and value, Heidegger believes that these are conferred on human existence by being.

But the starting point of the quest is man—the being who raises the question of being. As Heidegger puts it, being is an issue for man. In the first instance, his own being is an issue. Man does not come ready-made from the hands of nature, like a rock or even a tree or an animal. Man comes rather in the form of *possibility*. Out of this possibility, he has to decide what he will become. It is for this reason that Heidegger reserves the term "existence" exclusively for the being of man. To exist (Latin: *ex-sistere*) is to emerge, to stand forth out of the indefinite into a determinate mode of being. Every man therefore decides, within limits, about the question of his own being. But this being of the individual is never something isolated. In innumerable ways, it is linked to a wider context of being. Thus, if in the first instance it is the question of one's own being that forces itself upon one, this question almost inevitably leads into the question of being in the widest sense. One may also express this by saying that the *existential* question leads into the *ontological* question.

In *Being and Time,* Heidegger offers a detailed phenomenological analysis of human existence. His analysis begins with everyday existence; that is to say, the mode of existence which runs along the familiar routine paths. Heidegger believes that this mode of existence is for the most part inauthentic. Man does not really become himself in such existing, because instead of choosing and developing his possibilities, he finds that these are already chosen for him. In everyday existing, man conforms to patterns already laid down and adapts himself to tasks that are already determined. If human existence is constituted on the one hand by possibility, this possibility is always qualified by facticity. By "facticity" is meant the element of givenness in existence. No one ever confronts a wide-open field of possibility. Some things are already decided for him. This comes about in all kinds of ways—through genetic factors, through socioeconomic conditions, through historical events over which we have no control, through the past choices of others or of oneself. Everyone is already in a situation where some possibilities have been closed off. Heidegger likes to talk of being "thrown" into existence. It is in this thrown factical condition that the individual must lay hold on such possibilities as are still open to him. In everyday existing, these may be few.

Man's everyday relation to the world is constituted by a network of practical concerns. Heidegger rejects the view, so long prevalent in Western philosophy, that man is primarily a subject to which the world is added as its object, and with this he rejects also the view that man's distinctive function is thinking and his relation to the world is constituted primarily by thought. "I think, therefore I am" is too narrow a basis for philosophy, both because of its subjectivism and its intellectualism. The starting point for Heidegger is the concrete reality of being-in-the-world, a whole within which self and world are distinguishable but not separable; and it is practical concern, not abstract thought, which at the most primordial level is the bond between self and world. This means that the everyday world is an instrumental world. Whatever man comes across, he seeks to incorporate into his world by harnessing it to his concerns. This is the existential basis of the process which has culminated in technology. Man's relation to the instrumental world is an ambiguous one. Although he begins by transcending the world in his existence, he tends in his concern to fall back into it and to become another item in the world rather than the distinctive existent.

Just as there is no self apart from a world, so there is no self apart from other selves. Man is a being-with-others as well as a being-in-the-world. But his everyday being-with-others is just as ambiguous and inauthentic as his everyday being-in-the-world. Others are experienced as "they"—the vague, unidentified and unidentifiable collective mass. "They" set the standards and make the decisions. Rarely does the average person make a decision that is authentically his own. For the most part—and especially in the mass societies of today—he conforms to the impersonal demands of the public. He neither becomes himself nor does he form personal relations in any depth with other selves.

The being of man is summed up in the concept of care. Care is constituted by the tension between possibility and facticity, and to these is added the third factor of falling. This idea is reminiscent of the theological doctrine of a fall of man, and refers to the tendency of the existent to lose his distinctive self-determining mode of being as he becomes just another item in the world or another faceless member of the mass.

The possibility of an authentic existence is sketched out in opposition to these leveling and depersonalizing tendencies. The quest for authentic existence has its roots in the experience of anxiety. Heidegger is indebted to Kierkegaard in his understanding of this basic mood. Unlike our everyday worries and fears which are occasioned by particular threats within the world, authentic anxiety is aroused rather by man's total situation in the world. It is the malaise through which we become aware of the basic precariousness of the human condition. Anxiety in turn is closely connected with two further phenomena of existence, and it is primarily our response to these that will direct us toward authenticity or inauthenticity. These two phenomena are death and conscience. If anxiety has already aroused the uneasy feeling of not being at home in the familiar world of everyday routines and publicly created roles, it is death that holds out the inevitable prospect of separation from that world. In everyday existing, the thought of death is excluded. But to accept death and to live in the face of it is to know an eschatological dimension of existence. To live in the face of the end is to be liberated from petty tyrannies for one's own individual and unrepeatable possibilities. Conscience is the call within oneself to realize these possibilities. What is often taken to be conscience is simply the reflection of the rules which "they" have decreed for the conduct of life (the superego of Freud). The authentic conscience is different from this. It is each one's summons to his unique selfhood,

and—like Kierkegaard and Nietzsche before him—
Heidegger believes that this will often conflict with
the demands of conventional morality.

The analysis of human existence worked out in
Being and Time was to have provided the clue
toward the construction of a concept of being in
general. It is clear that this would have differed
markedly from traditional concepts. By taking the
being of man as the model rather than the being of
things, Heidegger turned away from any substantial
concept of thinghood to more dynamic concepts.
However, as we have already noted, his early way
toward understanding the meaning of being broke
off, and we come to the enigmatic work of the later
Heidegger.

A New Direction

The new direction is already indicated in Heidegger's famous inaugural lecture when he returned to
Freiburg in 1929. The lecture was entitled "What is
Metaphysics?" and consisted in the discussion of a
metaphysical question—the question of nothing.
Paradoxically, the "nothing" with which metaphysics
is concerned turns out to be "being." For being "is"
not a substance or another being in addition to those
which constitute the world. Yet it is more "beingful"
than any being. It is this "nothing which is also
being" of which one may become aware when, in the
mood of authentic anxiety, the world falls away.

Subsequent writings develop the notion of a thinking in which man is receptive to being. Such thinking
differs from the calculative thinking of everyday
existence in having a passive character. In some
respects, Heidegger's later philosophy seems to approach mysticism, but he himself stresses the parallel
with poetry. Language becomes increasingly im-

portant for his philosophy. Language is not a human invention but is the "house of being," the vehicle through which being reveals itself to the particular being who has been made its steward or shepherd, namely, man.

Heidegger's influence has been very great, not only on contemporary philosophy, but on psychiatry, education, historiography and, above all, theology. In the latter, his insights have been exploited by Bultmann, Tillich, and many others in their interpretations of man, revelation and God.

FOR FURTHER READING

Martin Heidegger, *Being and Time.*
———, *Introduction to Metaphysics* (Yale University Press).
———, *Discourse on Thinking* (Harper & Row).
John Macquarrie, *Martin Heidegger* (John Knox Press).

XI

Jürgen Moltmann

BY DANIEL L. MIGLIORE

Jürgen Moltmann is a leading spokesman of the theology of hope or eschatological theology. Eschatology means literally "the doctrine of the last things," and traditionally it dealt with events which were to occur at the end of time. Moltmann's theology is not eschatological in this traditional sense. Rather it focuses upon the "mobilizing, revolutionizing, and critical" impact of Christian hope on the present life of man.[1]

With recent "secular theology" Moltmann shares the vision of a creative worldly Christianity. And with "radical theology" he shares the conviction that the traditional models of transcendence, including that of neoorthodoxy, are seriously defective. What distinguishes Moltmann's work, however, from other prominent currents in contemporary theology is his interpretation of Christianity as essentially a world-transforming hope in a qualitatively new future.

DANIEL L. MIGLIORE teaches at Princeton Theological Seminary, Princeton, New Jersey.

[1] Jürgen Moltmann, *Theology of Hope* (New York: Harper & Row, 1967), p. 15.

At least three major influences on Moltmann's thought are readily apparent. The first is the biblical tradition read as the witness of a disturbing and creative hope evoked by the promise of God. The God of Israel continually calls his people into an unknown future. By his word of promise God keeps man unreconciled to the injustice and suffering of the present. The message and work of Jesus and the faith of the primitive Christian community belong in the explosive stream of prophetic hope. But again and again in its history the church has lost touch with this revolutionary messianic hope of the Bible and has simply conformed to the given state of affairs.

A second major influence on Moltmann is the neo-Marxist thought of Ernst Bloch whose philosophical masterpiece is entitled *The Principle of Hope*. Bloch views the world as unfinished and speaks of man as still in process of reaching his true identity. Hence in his philosophy the categories of "not-yet," future, and radical novelty are basic. Bloch credits the Bible for introducing the hope of a new world into the consciousness of man. Moltmann's celebrated book, *Theology of Hope* (1964), launches a theological program parallel to and in critical dialogue with Bloch's philosophy of hope.

The third obvious influence is the pervasive concern about the future in our time. Men today are both fascinated and terrified by the future and what it may bring. A new science of "futurology" is emerging which attempts to forecast various kinds of problems and to suggest alternative ways of dealing with them. In a very different vein from such scientific planning, social revolutionaries also want to create a new future for man. Moltman recognizes that we live in the midst of unsettling technological change and political upheaval, and he asks whether Christianity has any contribution to make to men in this situation.

Born in Germany in 1926, Moltmann is presently Professor of Systematic Theology at the University of Tübingen. In 1967–68 he taught in the United States and was impressed by the protest movements against the Vietnam war and racism in American society. After Auschwitz and as a German, Moltmann refuses to speak cheaply of hope. He likes to describe his theology of hope as an open theology of questions rather than a closed theology of answers. And he emphasizes that the point of his theology is not merely to interpret the world differently but to help to change it.

Hope and the Future of God

For Moltmann the God of the biblical witness is the creative power of the future. God is not a supernatural being "above" nor a given reality "within" man. God is "ahead" of man, "ahead of us in the horizons of the future opened to us in his promises." [2] God's promising word arouses man to a world-transforming hope. The exodus of Israel from bondage and the resurrection of the crucified Jesus are central biblical paradigms of the unsettling presence of God in the promise of a totally new reality.

Moltmann thus insists that to believe in God in the biblical sense is not to give a religious blessing to the status quo but to experience the present as in need of change. The transcendence of Christian hope is not otherworldly but works critically on the present. Authentic hope issues in historical change.

[2] Jürgen Moltmann, "Theology as Eschatology," in *The Future of Hope,* edited by Frederick Herzog (New York: Herder and Herder, 1970), p. 10.

What Moltmann calls the future of God is not to be identified with the future which is simply the extension of present reality. A distinction is necessary between the future understood as the realization of now available possibilities and the future understood as the coming of a surprising gift. With this distinction Moltmann offers a new model of transcendence. The activity of God is experienced not in the stubborn persistence of the same but in creative disruption and the coming of the new.

These two conceptions of the future correspond to two different ways of knowing and two different lifestyles. In the one case, the future is apprehended solely by analyzing already established trends and projecting them into the future. By this method the future is perceived as the field of quantitative but not of qualitative change. In the other case, man reaches toward the future in anticipation and creative imagination. He does not expect merely more of the same but the appearance of something genuinely new.

Similarly, there is a difference of ethical styles in relation to the future. In the one case, the future is seen as a purely human construction. This produces an intoxicating understanding of man and his responsibility for the future. But unless the future is approached in a spirit of hopeful confidence in the ultimate openness and graciousness of reality, creativity withers and man becomes prejudiced against the arrival of the new. Hence hope grounded in the future of God nurtures an ethical style which can wait as well as act and which is open to receive the future as a gift.

Real transcendence for Moltmann is experienced and practiced when men let go of old securities and take the risk of change in the direction of a new world of justice, freedom, and peace for all men.

Critics of Moltmann charge that his talk of God in terms of hope and the open future robs the past and present of significance. His response is that men really cherish the past only as they find in it still unfulfilled promises and possibilities. Hope alienates us only from the fossilized past and sets us in opposition to a present closed in on itself. Hope keeps the past and present of man alive because it apprehends them in terms of their promise of future fulfillment.

The new, Moltmann says, is not necessarily absolutely new. In his memory of promises unfulfilled, in his dreams of a better world, in his present experiences of suffering and of love there are advance notices of the future toward which man moves in hope. The life, death and resurrection of Jesus is affirmed by the Christian to be the decisive advance notice of God's coming new reality.

The Cross in Hope

Christian hope has come to be associated with otherworldliness. The message of the cross has often been rendered: "Endure all suffering and abuse without protest. Do not try to change conditions in this life but accept them as the cross you must bear." As a result, Moltmann contends, hope for the future of the earth has migrated from the church to various secular movements which view the church as the friend of the established powers and as the enemy of the oppressed. Faith in "God without hope" for this earth has been understandably opposed in the modern era by militant "hope without God."

Moltmann challenges the church to become an "exodus community" and to enter into a supportive as well as critical relationship to the authentic freedom movements of our time. In this spirit he has participated in the new Christian-Marxist dialogue in Europe. He holds that Christians can help to determine the spirit in which the future of the earth is sought only from a position of solidarity with the poor and the weak. Otherwise the needed critiques of revolutionary self-righteousness and legalism lack cogency.

Yet the church engaged in the struggle for human liberation would become completely superfluous if it did not bear its witness to the cross in hope. Hope prompts action, but the spirit of active Christian hope differs from the spirit of anarchy and terrorism. The future cannot be forced but must be approached in trust and sacrificial love. A more human future cannot be attained by adopting inhuman means.

Moltmann poses this basic question: Are we able to hope in the face of strong resistance and many disappointments without succumbing to the nihilism of despair or indiscriminate violence? Christian faith answers yes because it finds the source of hope in the cross of the risen Christ. The message of the cross is God's unconditional loyalty to the future of man and the earth. Because Christian hope is founded on the crucified Lord, it is not easily shaken. "Only through suffering and sacrifice does hope become clearsighted and sage. We have seen too many hopes disintegrate into resignation or violence at the first sign of resistance. Hope is the art of perseverance." [3]

The spirit of what Moltmann calls "crucified hope" reaches into both the personal and political dimensions of human life. Men must be willing to die to their isolated selves in order to find a new identity within a larger cause and a more inclusive horizon of meaning. Similarly, our institutions and social

[3] Jürgen Moltmann, "Politics and the Practice of Hope," *The Christian Century,* LXXXVII, No. 10 (March 11, 1970), p. 291.

structures, including those of the church, must be open to death to make way for new life. A church that is afraid of death and resists its own radical transformation in the service of man and his future betrays in its existence the gospel which it proclaims.

Hope prepares the way for love. For love is impossible without the willingness to expend ourselves for others. Hope gives us the freedom "to expend ourselves in love and in the work of reconciliation of the world with God and his future." [4]

The Theology of Hope as Political Theology

Moltmann's theology of hope is a political theology. Whereas recent existentialist theology has concentrated on the individual to the neglect of the larger social and natural milieu in which man lives, Moltmann insists that man's quest for personal identity and fulfillment is inseparably linked to his identification in hope with all men who suffer and long to be free and with all creation which "groans as in the pangs of childbirth" (Romans 8:22).

Moltmann's political theology does not disparage the significance of the person. It endeavors to bring the eschatological hope of Christianity to bear on the concrete world of social, political, and economic relationships in which each person exists. Abuse of our natural environment, for example, shows the bankruptcy of an individualistic understanding of man and his destiny. Whether we relate to nature as ruthless conquerors or as responsible stewards will depend on the inclusiveness of our hope and on our resolve to embody our hope in political action.

Moltmann observes that Americans historically have thought of freedom as freedom in space. Men simply moved west to find virgin land and to begin

[4] *Theology of Hope*, p. 337.

life anew. But Americans can no longer escape the burden of history in this way. The "new world," like the "old world," now has its own legacy of injustice and betrayed possibilities. Moltmann proposes that the idea of freedom in space be replaced by the pursuit of freedom in time. The world here and now must be transformed and made more human by combating economic, political and racial alienation.

A political theology of hope functions first of all as critic of those aspects of present society which demean man. The symbols of Christian expectation are expressions of protest against given social realities like racism and militarism. This is not to say that the Christian knows more about the future than do other men. But as he looks to the cross of Christ he knows what does *not* belong to the promised future of God. The Christian thus prepares the way for the arrival of the new by "negating the negative." He may not be able to say clearly what he means by "a new heaven and a new earth," but he knows and opposes the old heaven and the old earth of tyranny and exploitation.

But a theology of hope is a theology of the creative imagination as well as a theology of protest. Christian expectation should stimulate dreams and visions of new and more human social orders. Without a touch of abandon and fantasy, hope shrivels to the search for the least evil alternative. The spirit of Christian hope imagines and anticipates real possibilities which exceed the calculations of the "realists." If imagination without careful planning is impotent, planning without imagination is blind.

Play and festivity are closely related to vigorous hope and active imagination. With some justification Moltmann's thought has been criticized for being somewhat austere. On closer look, however, his theology invites a new spirit of playfulness. A theology of hope which stimulates creative imagination, play, and festivity may help to overcome the temptation of brutality and legalism in the search for a more just and free world. Moltmann suggests that one of the major contributions of Christians to the revolutions of our time may be to infect them with "the spirit of festivity and laughing" and thus help to transform revolution into permanent revolution.

FOR FURTHER READING

Jürgen Moltmann, "Politics and the Practice of Hope," *The Christian Century,* LXXXVII, No. 10 (March 11, 1970), pp. 288–91.

———, *Religion, Revolution and the Future* (New York: Charles Scribner's Sons, 1969). Read the "Author's Preface" and the essay "God in Revolution."

———, *Theology of Hope* (New York: Harper & Row, 1967). Try the introduction, "Meditation on Hope."

XII

Alfred North Whitehead

BY JOHN B. COBB, JR.

The Bible spoke powerfully about God, but what it had to say could not answer the questions of those whose minds were shaped by the intellectual quest and achievement of the Greeks. Christianity early recognized the need of speaking to these people, and to do so it absorbed much of the best of Greek thought into a creative synthesis. For a thousand years Platonic categories were dominant. Later the church turned to Aristotle.

The development of modern science raised questions about God that neither the Bible nor Greek philosophy could answer. Many new responses arose. Their tendency was to exclude God from immediate involvement with natural processes and to see him as much less directly available or relevant for human affairs than does the Bible. They also conflicted with each other. Whether any idea of God at all was needed or desirable became increasingly uncertain. With the rise of the new physics in the early twentieth century, all the familiar landmarks of thought gave

JOHN B. COBB, JR. is Ingraham Professor of Theology, School of Theology at Claremont, California.

way, and modern man generally gave up even asking the questions that led to discussion of God.

Nevertheless, in the nineteen-twenties a few speculative thinkers began putting together the pieces of a new cosmology. Evolutionary biology, relativity physics, field theory, and quantum mechanics were the main ingredients from the natural sciences. Problems in modern mathematics also required attention. The historical consciousness and depth psychology were important from the side of man's understanding of himself. Even extrasensory perception played a role.

The most successful product of this effort at a new synthesis was the philosophy of Alfred North Whitehead. He was born in 1861, shortly after his father had been ordained a clergyman of the Anglican Church. He studied at Cambridge and remained there as a teacher until 1910. He spent fourteen years in London and then, at the age of sixty-three, he began a new career at Harvard University. His great work of philosophical synthesis was done during these Harvard days and, partly as a result, its major influence has been in this country. Only recently have signs of serious interest in Whitehead appeared on the European continent, and even in England his late work has been but little studied until the last few years.

Like many, perhaps most, of the greatest thinkers of the West, Whitehead came to philosophy from mathematics. As a mathematician he had long wrestled with fundamental questions about the nature of algebra, geometry, and logic. He was keenly interested in the new physics and worked out a theory of relativity that may yet prove more precise in its mathematical predictions than that of Einstein. He moved on to a stupendous attempt to overcome the fragmentation of modern science and its separation from the inner life of man through a fundamental reconceptualization of reality.

Whitehead's Philosophy

The actual world, he asserted, is made up, not of bits of matter or patches of sense data but of atomic happenings, events, or occurrences, which he called *actual occasions*. Both the subelectronic quanta and momentary human experiences are examples of such occurrences. Each is an acting, feeling subject in the moment it takes place, and each then becomes an object which all those that follow must take into account. The difference between an acting subject and a passive object is the difference between the present and the past. There is no actual thing that in and of itself is always merely an object, as materialists and dualists suppose, and similarly there is no unchanging substance to which things happen. Also, there is no underlying subject who feels and acts. There are only happenings, which are also feelings and actions.

It is not easy to shift from our ordinary way of perceiving our world to this one. Furthermore, Whitehead's account is far more technical and intricate than these few sentences suggest. Hence, even professional philosophers find Whitehead difficult. When Whitehead gave the substance of *Process and Reality,* his most important book, as the Gifford Lectures of 1927–28, six hundred turned up to hear his first lecture. But thereafter only six returned! When Whitehead's followers try, as I am now trying, to express his ideas in a way that can be more easily understood, they often lose the very heart of his vision. Whitehead does not primarily offer new solutions to widely recognized problems. Rather he undertakes a fundamental reconstruction of our culturally shaped common sense. One cannot enter into the new vision he offers us in six easy lessons! But there is reason to think it may play a much larger role in the future.

In addition to the endless flux of the seething multiplicity that is the actual world, there is the eternal, unchanging realm of pure possibility. This is the realm in which Whitehead, along with his fellow mathematicians, had been absorbed. Whitehead was immensely impressed by the unfathomable range of possibility. In comparing what actually happens with the unlimited variety of things that *might* happen, he became aware that the becoming of new occasions required a *principle of limitation*. Each occurrence arises out of the teeming multitude of past events. This past provides most of its content. But there can be no new occurrence except as there is selection from this past. For example, my present experience cannot include all the content of my past experiences along with the new material provided by my senses. It must select, and that selection is guided by some purpose. The purpose is directed toward some value. The attraction of this value is thus the center around which the new experience comes to be. Since each occurrence has a different context, each must be attracted toward a different value. This value must be relevant for it, and it must be appropriate to the maintenance of a general order that will allow later occurrences to attain their measure of value as well. It must introduce novelty without disrupting the process. Hence, the principle of limitation is that factor in the whole by virtue of which there is ordered novelty and novel order. It is the ground of what we rather misleadingly call "scientific laws" or "the laws of nature." It is the source of life and growth and

of the drive toward greater intensities of feeling and
wider ranges of involvement and concern. Apart
from it, if there were anything at all, it would be
that world described by the second law of thermo-
dynamics—a world decaying into less and less interesting forms of order and randomness, toward
what is called heat death.

The expression "principle of limitation" sounds
negative and restrictive. That is not Whitehead's
view, since limitation is the price of definiteness, and
without definiteness there is no actuality. Only pure
possibility can be unlimited, and the slightest whiff
of actuality is of more intrinsic value than the entire
realm of possibility. The principle of limitation is
therefore "the principle of concretion." Whitehead
also calls it "Eros" and "the primordial nature of
God."

Whitehead as Theologian

The introduction of God into his philosophy cost
Whitehead a good deal of support in the philosophic
community. In the climate of that time the prejudice
against theism was so strong that Whitehead's speaking of God was taken as an indication that he must
be growing senile. It won him little support among
theologians, for they were busily engaged in separating what the Christian means by "God" from anything that can be known apart from revelation, and
especially from philosophical concepts and principles.
Nevertheless, the introduction of "God" was by no
means casual or careless. It was not an arbitrary
designation of some concept needed to complete his
system. Whitehead was convinced that this ultimately
decisive factor in the whole of reality is that which
has elicited the worship of man's great religions.
Philosophy can tell us only a little about this reality.

The religious intuitions and experiences of gifted men tell us more. Actual religious experience can and should clothe the abstract concept with concreteness and imaginative reality.

But even what philosophy alone establishes is religiously important. God, as the source of the purpose around which each momentary occurrence comes into being, does not rigidly determine what that occurrence must become. The decision belongs to the occurrence. God's work in the world is to persuade it to actualize whatever good it can. The world, and each of us, responds by some partial realization of the ideal possibility and by some partial failure. God responds in his turn by luring us toward the new possibility that results from the new situation. God's gift is the context of our freedom. How we exercise our freedom determines what gift can next be given. Whitehead thus points toward a resolution of the traditional tension between divine grace and human freedom. Each requires and presupposes the other.

There is another side of Whitehead's doctrine of God that is equally important for Christian thought. Each of the occurrences making up the world is related both to its past world and to new possibilities. Whitehead calls the relation to the past world the physical pole and the relation to possibility the mental pole. Thus everything whatsoever is both physical and mental. Human experience is in part "physical," and an electronic event is in part "mental." The difference is a matter of degree, however great it may be. Whitehead further holds that God cannot be an exception to metaphysical requirements of this sort. This means that in addition to his primordial nature, which is God's mental pole, God must have also a physical pole. Whitehead calls the physical pole of God his "consequent nature." The consequent nature is God's experience of the world.

Real relations, Whitehead teaches, are always the relations of subjects to objects; that means, of what is now in the act of becoming to what has already become. What has become enters into the new process of becoming. Consequently, as each of our experiences passes, it is taken up into God's ever-lasting experience of us. In and through God we have everlasting life. For this reason the ceaselessly passing and perishing occasions have not merely the ephemeral value of the moment but also *importance*. What happens matters *now* because it matters *ever-lastingly*.

Whitehead can write quite literally that God is in the world and that the world is in God. God contributes to the world and the world contributes to God. There is a permanence both about God and about the world, and both God and the world are in process of becoming. The traditional contrasts of God's immutability and the world's mutability, God's eternality and the world's temporality, God's absoluteness and the world's relativity are transcended, and with them many of the puzzles of traditional theism. In some respects Christian liturgy and piety along with the New Testament understanding of God are vindicated against traditional philosophical theology, which was deeply affected by Greek categories. God really is concerned about the world in all its details and even suffers with us in our suffering. What we are and do really makes a difference to God. Love really is the key to our understanding of God.

Whitehead's doctrine of God differs from the more widely held Protestant positions since Kant by relating God not only to history and morality and religion, but also to nature and science. This is one mark of his overcoming of the dualism of the human and the subhuman world. But that has importance for Protestant thought in other ways as well. Whitehead shows us man as a part of nature without denying his distinctiveness or the importance of his history. Consciousness is a limited aspect of special types of experience possible only in the higher organisms with their more complex nervous systems, but it is not cut off from nature as something outside of it. Human experience affects the bodily experiences out of which it arises, and the interaction of human and other occasions extends throughout nature. The interdependence of man and his environment replaces the estrangement and dualism of much modern thought. Respect for all levels of being replaces the spirit of conquest. Kinship and stewardship rather than domination and casual exploitation express the relation to the environment appropriate to Whitehead's vision.

Most Western philosophies and theologies have thought of man as having or being a substantial, underlying soul or self. This has encouraged a strong individualism which in turn has tended to isolate each man from his neighbor. We have disparaged our susceptibility to being shaped by others as a form of weakness or inauthenticity.

Whitehead denies a substantial soul. There are instead numerous occurrences, each of which is an experience growing out of past experiences and passing on their enriched inheritance to the future. The personal individuality achieved by Western man is a great attainment, but it need not be an end. Each occurrence of human experience inherits from the experiences of others as well as from a man's own past. Through heightened sensitivity and greater openness to others, receptivity can be enhanced. Deepened interaction can produce a communal man who retains his individual personhood but who, by giving and receiving in love, breaks out of the rigidity and isolation that have been involved in Western individualism.

Whitehead is useful for theology in yet another way. The context for Christian reflection has become the history of all the world's religions. He himself saw Buddhism and Christianity as the two most serious claimants for man's religious commitment, and he incorporated elements of both in his philosophy of religion. It is not surprising, therefore, that Buddhists as well as other Orientals find much that is congenial in Whitehead's philosophy. It is not a syncretism of the several religions, but it provides relatively neutral concepts in terms of which each can be appreciatively understood and responsibly criticized. It can help Christians to transcend the parochialism of their past and to be enriched by the insights of other traditions without surrendering their own unique and distinctive faith. But for the most part this remains yet to be done.

An Alternative

In the current theological and cultural climate there is a deep tension between those who cling to the past and those who would cut loose from that past and live purely out of the future. Whitehead offers an alternative far more promising than either. Against those who would cling to the past he warns us that the past is perished and there is no return. It is not possible to repeat the past, and we should not try to do so. However great the value of the past may have been, to whatever degree repetition dominates, zest and vitality are lost. Novelty is needed not only when the past is bad but also when it is good; for a stale good quickly becomes evil.

Against those who would cut loose from the past he insists that all present realization arises out of the past. Each occasion comes into being as a selective synthesis of elements from the past. There is no other way to become at all—even for God! The more of the past one can incorporate, the greater the possibilities for present value.

The error of those who perceive the past as a burden to be cast off rather than as a resource is their supposition that the more we are shaped by the past the less we can embody the novel possibilities of the future. In fact, however, the reverse is the case. Just those occasions that appropriate the past most richly have the greatest freedom in their own self-constitution and introduce the greatest novelty. It is just because a human being through memory and language and depth of feeling brings so much of the past into each new moment that he can realize so much more of freedom and novelty than can a dog. No one can really cut himself off from his past, but to whatever extent he reduces its contribution to his present experience he condemns himself to dull repetition and routine. To conserve as much as possible through active selection and to share in the creative advance into novelty belong together. They jointly constitute the optimum response to the divine persuasion.

Whitehead as philosopher did not develop a Christology. Yet he has helped us here also. He saw that Christianity is centered around a few crucial events. The teaching of Jesus is at the lowest level of abstraction at which language can be language. Thus Christianity is not essentially a theory about the world but the inspiration of a life and message. Its need is a conceptuality that can interpret the whole of things in the light of the insights to which it is committed. Whitehead's philosophy can itself be viewed as fulfilling Christian faith in this way. Philosophy is thus not a replacement of faith but its complement.

Whiteheadian theologians have taken their clue for Christology here, but the possibilities are still undeveloped. They have reflected on how Jesus' message and person present in a focused way the gracious action of God everywhere in the world, but they have considered very little the quite particular ways in which the God who acts everywhere was present in Jesus and how Jesus has shaped the history of the world. More important, in their concern to speak with literal precision, they have paid too little attention to the Christ symbol, the Christ of the believer's imagination, whose importance for history and faith is no less than that of the historical Jesus. Whitehead has richly analyzed the place and effective reality of such symbols and images, but the theological task of appropriating Whitehead here remains to be carried out.

Through most of Christian history, theology and philosophy have been closely wed. After World War I theology decided on a trial separation, partly because her partner had been so often unfaithful. That separation has led to many difficulties, and there are now signs that, rather than going on to a final divorce, theology is ready to renew the marriage. A growing group of theologians is convinced that Whitehead offers the last best hope for this new try.

FOR FURTHER READING

A. N. Whitehead, *Adventure of Ideas* (Cambridge University Press, 1933).

————, *Process and Reality* (Cambridge University Press, 1927).

————, *Religion in the Making* (Cambridge University Press, 1926).

————, *Science and the Modern World* (Cambridge University Press, 1936).

John B. Cobb, Jr., *A Christian Natural Theology* (Westminster Press, 1965).

Norman Pittenger, *Process Thought and Christian Faith* (Macmillan, 1968).

Schubert Ogden, *The Reality of God* (Harper & Row, 1967).

Daniel Day Williams, *The Spirit and the Forms of Love* (Harper & Row, 1968).